Renaissance

SCALA

Contents

Inhalt

Index

Inhoudsopgave

Introduction

The Renaissance, a vast cultural and ideological movement, was the period of intense literary, artistic and scientific creativity that involved Europe between the 14th and 16th centuries and marked the transformation from the medieval to a modern concept of the intellect. During the early Renaissance, focused and nurtured in Florence and in Italy, the arts and culture underwent a radical renewal that spread gradually across Europe by various means and stylistic expressions. The Renaissance was based on the renewed passion for the ancient world – from philosophy to literature, from mythology to art – Neo-Platonic philosophy and humanism. Scientific interests included research into Nature and the human being such as anatomical studies and the exploration of new techniques, while the harmonious union of the major arts rose above the level of mechanical reproduction to become a free expression of the now consolidated intellectual prerogatives of the artist. Some of the great names that made this artistic season so fertile are Masaccio, Brunelleschi, Leonardo, Michelangelo, Raffaello, the Flemish masters Van Eyck and Van der Weyden, the artists of the school of Fontainebleau and the German painters Dürer, Altdorfer and Holbein. The fundamental contribution of the courts, lords, patrons and men of the church who used the new stylistic languages to embellish their manors and estates was a natural consequence of the splendour of the arts.

Einleitung

Die weitreichende ideologische und kulturelle Bewegung der Renaissance stellte eine bedeutende Blütezeit für Literatur, Kunst und Wissenschaft dar, begeisterte zwischen dem 14. und 16. Jhdt n. Chr. ganz Europa und besiegelte den Übergang vom mittelalterlichen Gedankengut zu einer neuen modernen Sichtweise. Vitales Zentrum der Frührenaissance war Italien, Florenz ihr Mittelpunkt, Künste und Kultur erlebten eine radikale Erneuerung, die sich nach und nach auf europäischer Skala in verschiedenem Ausmaß und allerlei Stilformen verbreitete. Zur Renaissance gehörten eine neue Liebe zur Welt der Antike – von der Philosophie zur Literatur, von der Mythologie zur Kunst – der Neuplatonismus und der Humanismus. Das wissenschaftliche Interesse weitete sich auf die Darstellung der Natur und des Menschen aus, unter anderem über die Anatomie, das Ausloten neuer Techniken und einer harmonischen Verbindung der Kunstrichtungen, die nicht mehr "mechanisch" sondern "liberal" waren und sich mit den bereits anerkannten intellektuellen Fähigkeiten des Künstlers schmückten. Zu den großen Namen, die zur Unsterblichkeit dieser Kunstepoche beitrugen, gehören Masaccio, Brunelleschi, Leonardo, Michelangelo, Raffael, die niederländischen Meister Van Eyck und Van der Weyden, die Künstler der Schule von Fontainebleau und die deutschen Maler Dürer, Altdorfer und Holbein. Mit dem Glanz der Künste war der maßgebliche Beitrag der Höfe, der Herrscher, der Mäzene und der Geistlichen verbunden, die mit den neuen Ausdrucksformen Wohnsitze und Länder bereicherten.

Introduction

La Renaissance, vaste mouvement idéologique et culturel, est une période de grand épanouissement littéraire, artistique et scientifique qui affecta l'Europe du XIVe au XVIe siècle, sanctionnant le passage de la pensée médiévale à une conception moderne de l'art et de la spiritualité. La première Renaissance voit se développer son principe moteur en Italie et en particulier à Florence : les arts et la culture y connaissent alors un renouveau radical qui se diffuse progressivement à l'échelle européenne, sous des identités et déclinaisons stylistiques diverses. Les piliers de cette Renaissance sont la redécouverte et l'amour du monde antique (de la philosophie à la littérature et de l'art à la mythologie), la philosophie néo-platonicienne et la culture humaniste. L'intérêt scientifique s'étend aux recherches sur la nature et sur l'être humain : s'y conjuguent entre autres l'anatomie, la mise au point de nouvelles techniques, et l'union harmonieuse entre les arts majeurs qui étaient « mécaniques » et deviennent « libéraux », en se prévalant des facultés désormais reconnues de l'artiste. Parmi les grands noms qui font briller cette période d'un éclat sans pareil se distinguent ceux de Masaccio, Brunelleschi, Donatello, Léonard de Vinci, Michel-Ange et Raphaël en Italie ; de Van Eyck et Van der Weyden dans les Flandres ; des artistes de l'École de Fontainebleau en France ; de Schongauer, Grünewald, Dürer, Altdorfer et Holbein en Allemagne. La splendeur des arts est également liée au mécénat éclairé des cours, des seigneurs et des princes de l'Église qui enrichissent leurs résidences et leurs territoires de toutes ces expressions nouvelles.

Introductie

De Renaissance, grote ideologische en culturele beweging, was een periode van grote literaire, artistieke en wetenschappelijke groei, die Europa trof tussen de 14e en de 16e eeuw, wat de overgang van het middeleeuwse denkbeeld naar een nieuwe moderne visie bezegelde. Tijdens de eerste Renaissance, die haar verspreidingscentrum in Italië en haar kern in Florence had, kende de kunst en de cultuur een radicale vernieuwing, die zich progressief verspreidde op Europese schaal, met diverse entiteiten en stilistische declinaties. Onder de Renaissance vallen de vernieuwde liefde voor de antieke oudheid – van de filosofie tot aan de literatuur en van de mythologie tot aan de kunst – de neoplatonische filosofie en de humanistische cultuur. De wetenschappelijke interesse breidt zich uit tot de oorsprong van de natuur en het menselijk wezen, onder andere door middel van de anatomie, het onderzoek naar nieuwe technieken en de harmonische vereniging tussen de arti maggiori (hogere ambachten), die van "mechanisch" veranderden in "vrij", afgewerkt door de inmiddels erkende intellectuele capaciteit van de kunstenaar. Onder de grote namen die het artistieke seizoen van deze periode lieten schitteren, vallen Brunelleschi, Leonardo, Michelangelo en Rafaël, de Vlaamse meesters Van Eyck en Van der Weyden, de kunstenaars van de school van Fontainebleau en de Duitse schilders Dürer, Altdorfer en Holbein. De pracht en praal van de kunsten zijn verbonden aan de toonaangevende bijdrage van de hoven, heren, mecenassen en eclecticisten, die verblijven en territoria verrijkten met de nieuwe stijlen.

The Renaissance Centres
Die Zentren der Renaissance
Les centres de la Renaissance
De centra van de Renaissance

ANTWERPEN

Philipp Oyrl
Fembohaus
1591-1596

Château de
Fontainebleau
1522-1540

FONTAINEBLEAU

Donato Bramante
Santa Maria delle Grazie
1492-1495

Giulio Romano
Palazzo Te
1524-1540

Biagio Rossetti
Palazzo dei Diamanti
1493-1503

Luciano Laurana
Palazzo Ducale
1466-1472

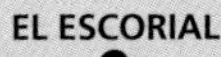

EL ESCORIAL

Juan Bautista de Toledo
Monasterio de San Lorenzo
1563-1585

Cornelis Floris de Vriendt
Stadhuis
1564
PRAHA
NÜRNBERG
Benedikt Ried
Stary Kralovsky palac
Vladislavsky sal
1493-1502
VISEGRAD
Château
1400-1500
Andrea Palladio
San Giorgio Maggiore
1566-1567
MILANO
VENEZIA
MANTOVA
FERRARA
FIRENZE
URBINO
Michelozzo
Palazzo Medici
1444-1452
Michelangelo Buonarroti
San Pietro
Cúpula / Cupola / Dome
1546-1564
Città del Vaticano
ROMA
NAPOLI
Francesco Laurana
Arco di Trionfo di Alfonso I
d'Aragona
1446-1451

1

Architecture in Italy

The Italian Renaissance produced remarkable results in architecture, among the highest in Europe. Between the fifteenth and sixteenth centuries artists such as Brunelleschi, Bramante, Alberti and Michelangelo constructed public and religious buildings and aristocratic dwellings, influenced by classic models and based on the most recent rules of perspective. They are noteworthy for the harmonious union of the individual parts, alternating essentiality and elegance, monumental mass and dynamic movement.

Architektur in Italien

Die Architektur der italienischen Renaissance erzielt bemerkenswerte Ergebnisse, die in Europa zu den besten zählen. Zwischen dem 15. und 16. Jhdt. realisieren Künstler wie Brunelleschi, Alberti und Michelangelo weltliche, religiöse und aristokratische Bauten, die von den klassischen Modellen beeinflusst und auf der Basis neuester Regeln der Perspektive strukturiert sind. Ihr Merkmal ist die harmonische Verbindung einzelner Teile, wobei sich Wesentlichkeit und Eleganz, Monumentalität und Dynamismus abwechseln.

L'architecture en Italie

La Renaissance italienne trouve dans l'architecture une expression dont les réalisations sont parmi les plus hautes d'Europe. Entre le XVe et le XVIe siècle, des artistes comme Brunelleschi, Bramante, Alberti et Michel-Ange créent des édifices civils, religieux et aristocratiques influencés par les modèles de l'Antiquité classique et structurés selon les règles perspectives les plus récentes. Ces bâtiments se distinguent par la fusion harmonieuse de leurs différentes parties, alternant élégance et fonctionnalité, monumentalité et dynamisme.

Architectuur in Italië

De Italiaanse Renaissance uit zich aanzienlijk in de architectuur en geldt als de beste van Europa. Tussen de vijftiende en de zestiende eeuw verwezenlijken kunstenaars als Brunelleschi, Bramante, Alberti en Michelangelo civiele, religieuze en aristocratische gebouwen, die beïnvloed zijn door klassieke en structurele modellen op basis van de nieuwste perspectiefregels. Ze kenmerken zich door de harmonieuze samenkomst van losstaande delen, afgewisseld met noodzakelijkheid en elegantie, monumentaliteit en dynamisme.

Filippo Brunelleschi
(Firenze 1377 - 1446)
Ospedale degli Innocenti
1418-1427
Firenze

▶ **Filippo Brunelleschi**
(Firenze 1377 - 1446)
Santa Maria del Fiore
Dome
Blick auf die Kuppel
Vue de la coupole
Koepelaanzicht
1420-1438
Firenze

▮ *"[Brunelleschi's dome is] A grandiose structure, as high as the heavens, and broad enough to wrap all the peoples of Tuscany in its shadow."*
▮ *"[Die Kuppel von Brunelleschi ist] Eine so grandiose Struktur am Himmel, so riesig, dass sie mit ihrem Schatten alle toskanischen Völker bedeckt."*
▮ *« [La coupole de Brunelleschi est] Une structure si grande, tournée vers les cieux, assez vaste pour couvrir de son ombre tous les peuples de la Toscane. »*
▮ *"[De koepel van Brunelleschi is] Een grootse structuur die zich opricht tot aan de hemel, zo immens, dat het met zijn schaduw de gehele Toscaanse bevolking bedekt."*
Leon Battista Alberti

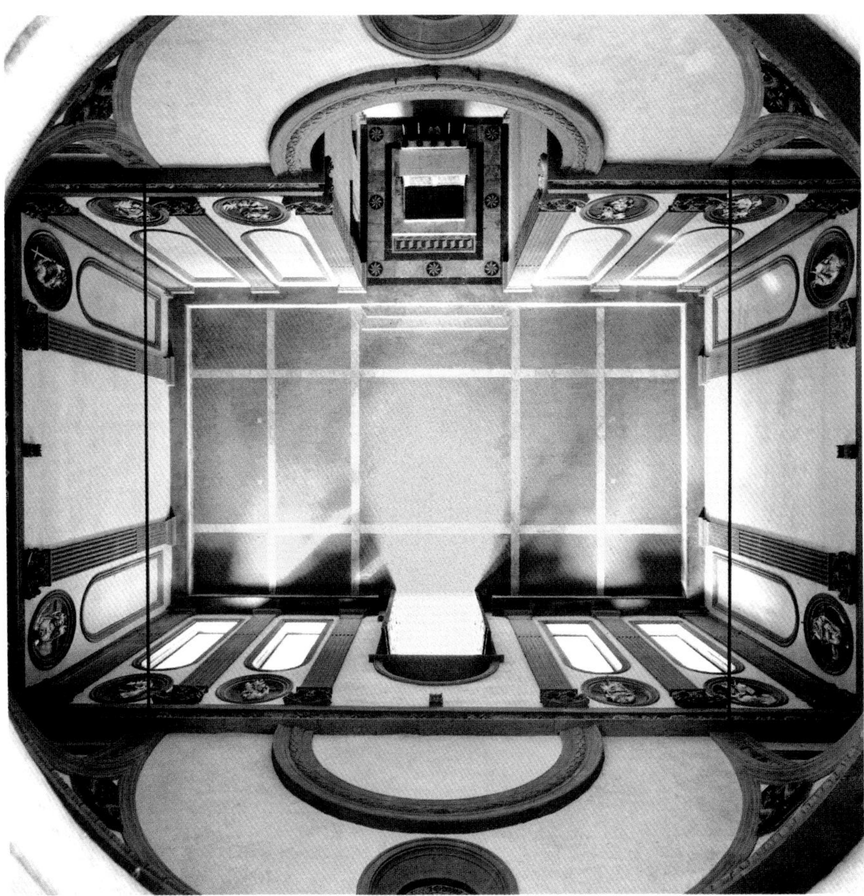

Filippo Brunelleschi
(Firenze 1377 - 1446)
Cappella dei Pazzi
View of the interior, from above
Das Innere von oben gesehen
Intérieur vu d'en haut
Interieuraanzicht vanaf boven
1429-1444
Firenze

◀ **Filippo Brunelleschi**
(Firenze 1377 - 1446)
San Lorenzo
Nave
Blick in das Innere
Vue de l'intérieur
Binnenaanzicht
1421-1428
Firenze

Leon Battista Alberti
(Genova 1406 - Roma 1472)
Tempio Malatestiano
Façade and right flank
Blick auf die Fassade und die rechte Seite
Vue de la façade et du côté droit
Aanzicht van de voorgevel en de rechterzijde
1450
Rimini

▶ **Leon Battista Alberti**
(Genova 1406 - Roma 1472)
Santa Maria Novella
Façade
Blick auf die Fassade
Vue de la façade
Voorgevelaanzicht
1456-1470
Firenze

"Architect I will call the man who will demonstrate with secure and marvellous rationale and rule, with both the mind and the spirit, to know how to section the portions."
"Architekt werde ich jenen nennen, der mit sicherem und feinem Verstand, mit der Regel, mit dem Geist und mit der Seele einzuteilen versteht."
« J'appellerai architecte celui qui saura diviser avec sûre et merveilleuse raison, et avec règle, mais aussi avec son âme et son esprit. »
"Ik zou een ieder architect noemen, die met zekere en uitstekende rede en regels en met geest en ziel weet te onderscheiden."
Leon Battista Alberti

IOHANES ORICELLARIVS PAV F AN SAL MCCCCLXX

Michelangelo Buonarroti
(Caprese, Arezzo 1475 - Roma 1564)
Biblioteca Medicea Laurenziana
Hall
Das Innere des Saals
Intérieur de la grande salle
Interieur van de Salon
1524-1534
Firenze

◀ **Benedetto da Maiano**
(Maiano, Firenze 1442 - Firenze 1497)
Simone del Pollaiolo
(Firenze 1457 - 1508)
Palazzo Strozzi
Façade and right flank
Blick auf die Fassade und die rechte Seite
Vue de la façade et du côté droit
Aanzicht van de voorgevel en van de rechterzijde
1489-1504
Firenze

Donato Bramante
(Fermignano, Pesaro 1444 - Roma 1514)
Spiral staircase
Blick auf die Wendeltreppe
Vue de l'escalier hélicoïdal
Aanzicht van de wenteltrap
c. 1512
Museo Pio-Clementino, Città del Vaticano

◀ **Donato Bramante**
(Fermignano, Pesaro 1444 - Roma 1514)
Tempietto
1502-1507
San Pietro in Montorio, Roma

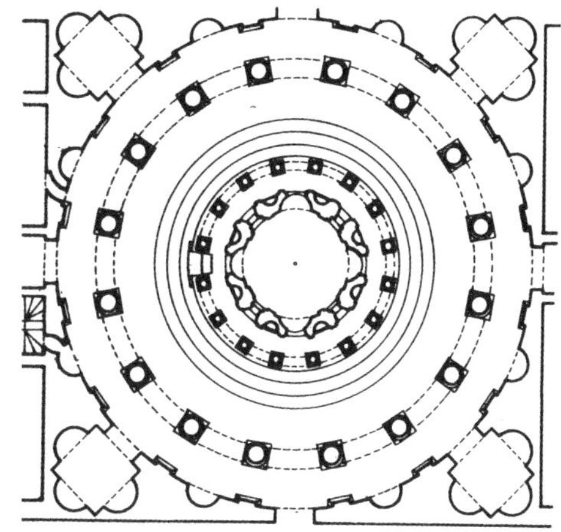

Pirro Ligorio
(Napoli c. 1510 - Ferrara 1583)
Cortile della Pigna
Great niche of Bramante
Blick auf die große Nische bekannt als Bramante
Vue de la niche de Bramante
Aanzicht van de "Nicchione", begonnen door Bramante
1562-1565
Palazzi Vaticani, Città del Vaticano

◀ **Michelangelo Buonarroti**
(Caprese, Arezzo 1475 - Roma 1564)
Basilica di San Pietro
Dome
Blick auf die Kuppel
Vue de la coupole
Koepelaanzicht
1546-1564

Antonio Rizzo
(Verona *c.* 1430 - Cesena 1499)
Pietro Lombardo
(Carona, Lugano 1435 - Venezia 1515)
Palazzo Ducale
Courtyard
Blick auf den Hof
Vue de la cour intérieure
Aanzicht van de binnenplaats
1484-1511
Venezia

◀ **Venezia**
Ca' d'Oro
Façade
Blick auf die Fassade
Vue de la façade
Voorgevelaanzicht
1422-1440

Andrea Palladio
(Padova 1508 - Maser, Treviso 1580)
Vincenzo Scamozzi
(Vicenza 1552 - Venezia 1616)
San Giorgio Maggiore
1566-1610
Venezia

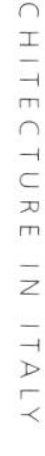

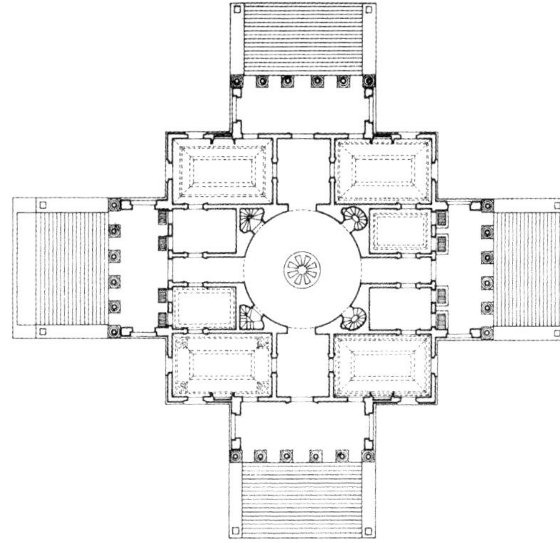

Andrea Palladio
(Padova 1508 - Maser, Treviso 1580)
La Rotonda
1566-1567
Vicenza

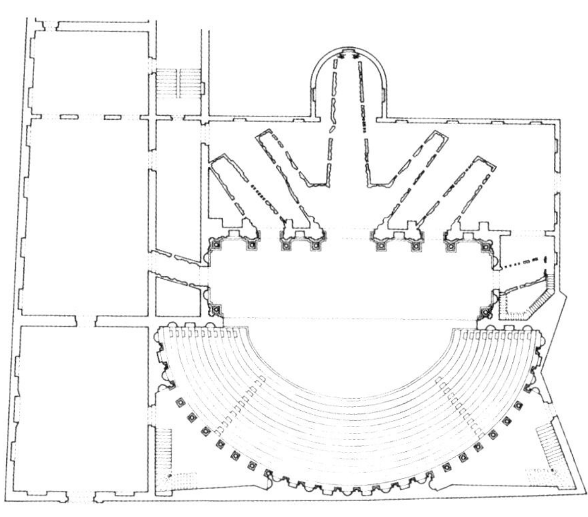

Andrea Palladio
(Padova 1508 - Maser, Treviso 1580)
Teatro Olimpico
Proscenium
Blick in Richtung Bühne
Vue de l'avant-scène
Aanzicht van de frons scenae
1580
Vicenza

◀ Vincenzo Scamozzi
(Vicenza 1552 - Venezia 1616)
Teatro all'antica
1588
Sabbioneta, Mantova

Giulio Romano
(Roma 1499 - Mantova 1546)
Palazzo Te
1524-1540
Mantova

Biagio Rossetti
(Ferrara *c.* 1447 - 1516)
Palazzo dei Diamanti
c. 1493-1503
Ferrara

Architecture in Europe

From Italy Renaissance architecture spread out to France and then to the rest of Europe, marking the end of the Gothic style and introducing new stylistic and engineering solutions. Among the most significant buildings, created with new concepts of beauty, harmony and proportion, the elegant and imposing castles built in France by François I, and the very famous, and just as austere, Escorial built in Spain by Philip II, are particularly outstanding.

Architektur in Europa

Von Italien aus verbreitet sich die Renaissance-Architektur zuerst nach Frankreich, dann in den Großteil Europas, setzt dem vorherrschenden gotischen Stil ein Ende und nähert sich den neuen stilistischen und technischen Lösungen. Zu den bemerkenswertesten Gebäuden, die im Sinne einer neuen Optik der Schönheit, Harmonie und Proportion errichtet werden, gehören z.B. die eleganten und eindrucksvollen französischen Schlösser unter Franz I. sowie der berühmte und stolze Bau des Escorial in Spanien auf Auftrag von Philip II.

2

L'architecture en Europe

Partant de l'Italie, l'architecture Renaissance se diffuse d'abord en France puis dans une grande partie de l'Europe, mettant fin au primat du style gothique «international» et instaurant de nouvelles solutions d'ingénierie et de style. Parmi les édifices les plus caractéristiques érigés dans cette nouvelle idée de beauté, d'harmonie et de proportion, se distinguent par exemple les palais et les châteaux construits en France sous François Ier, et l'ensemble aussi célèbre qu'austère de l'Escorial, voulu en Espagne par Philippe II, le fils de Charles Quint.

Architectuur in Europa

De Renaissancistische architectuur breidde zich vanuit Italië, eerst uit naar Frankrijk en daarna naar de meeste andere delen van Europa, het einde van de recordhoudende Gotische stijl inluidend en de nieuwe stilistische en technische oplossingen invoerend. Onder de meest kenmerkende gebouwen, die zijn opgericht volgens de vernieuwde optiek van schoonheid, harmonie en afmetingen, vallen bijvoorbeeld de elegante en indrukwekkende Franse kastelen, die onder het beheer van Frans I vielen en het beroemde en trotse Escorial in Spanje, opgedragen door Filips II.

Philibert Delorme
(Lyon c. 1510 - Paris 1570)
Château de Chenonceaux
1556-1559

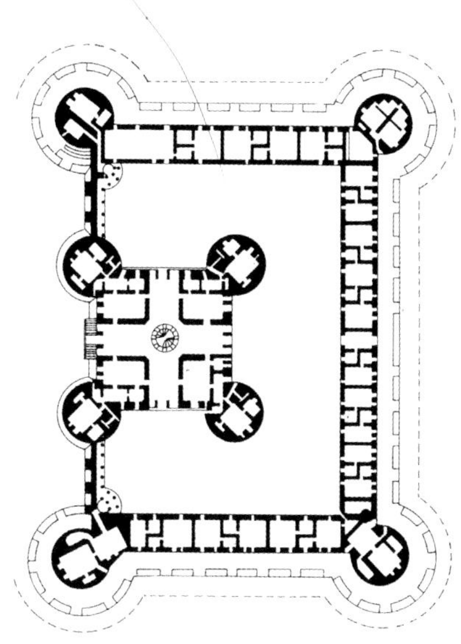

Château de Chambord
1519-1537

Château de Fontainebleau
Cour du Cheval blanc
Blick auf den Hof von Cheval-Blanc
Vue de la cour du Cheval blanc
Aanzicht van de binnenplaats van Cheval-Blanc
*c.*1542

◀ Château de Fontainebleau
Galerie François Ier
1522-1540

Juan Guas
(Saint-Pol-de-Léon, Finistère 1430? - Toledo 1496)
Castillo de los Mendoza
c. 1475
Manzanares el Real

▶ **Burgos**
Cathedral
Kathedrale
Cathédrale
Kathedraal
Capilla del Condestable
1400-1500

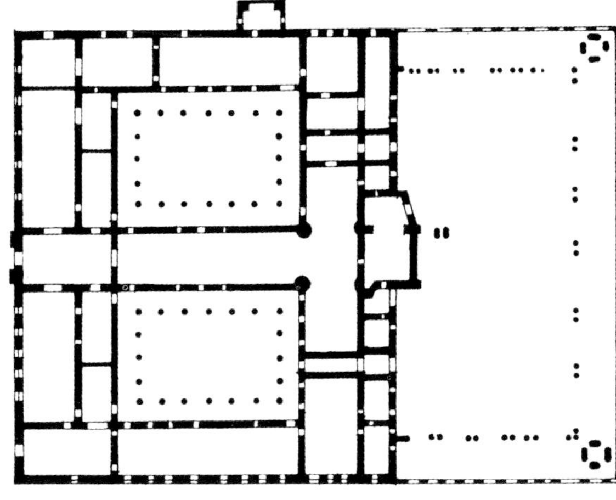

Enrique de Egas
(Toledo *c.* 1455 - 1534)
Hostal de los Reyes Católicos
Detail of the façade
Detail der Fassade
Détail de la façade
Detail van de voorgevel
c. 1501
Santiago de Compostela

Diego de Siloé
(Burgos c. 1495 - Granada 1563)
Escalera dorada
Cathedral
Kathedrale
Cathédrale
Kathedraal
1519-1526
Burgos

Pedro Machuca
(Toledo1485 - Granada 1550)
Palacio de Carlos V
Courtyard
Blick auf den Innenhof
Vue de la cour intérieure
Aanzicht van de patio
1526-1550
Granada

◀ **Diego de Siloé**
(Burgos c. 1495 - Granada 1563)
Capilla Mayor
Cathedral
Kathedrale
Cathédrale
Kathedraal
1528-1559
Granada

Juan Bautista de Toledo
(Toledo c. 1515 - Madrid 1567)
Monasterio de San Lorenzo
1563-1585
El Escorial

Juan Bautista de Toledo
(Toledo c. 1515 - Madrid 1567)
Monasterio de San Lorenzo
Library
Bibliothek
Bibliothèque
Bibliotheek
1563-1585
El Escorial

Maestro Huguet
Mosteiro de Santa Maria da Vitória
Capelas Imperfeitas
Interior
Innenansicht
Intérieur
Interieur
1434-1438
Batalha

▶ **Diogo de Torralva**
Convento da Ordem de Cristo
Great cloister
Großes Kloster
Grand cloître
Grote Klooster
c. 1550
Tomar

Diogo de Boitaca
(*c.* 1460 - Batalha 1528?)
João de Castilho
(? - *c.* 1553)
Mosteiro dos Jerónimos de Belém
Cloister
Kloster
Cloître
Klooster
1550-1600
Lisboa

Francisco de Arruda
(? - 1547)
Torre de Belém
1515-1521
Lisboa

Anno
1535
Schiffer-Gesellschaft
GOTTESKELLER
Breite Straße

Heidelberg
Schloss, Friedrichsbau
c. 1592

◀ **Lübeck**
Schiffergesellschaft
1535

Moscow
Cathedral of the Annunciation, façade
Verkündigungs-Kathedrale, Blick auf die Fassade
Cathédrale de l'Annonciation, vue de la façade
Kathedraal van de Annunciatie, voorgevelaanzicht
1484-1489

► **Postnik Yakovlev**
(1524-1612)
Cathedral of St. Basil, view of the domes
Basilius-Kathedrale, Detail der Kuppeln
Cathédrale Saint-Basile, détail des coupoles
Kathedraal van San Basilio, detail van de koepel
1555-1561
Moscow

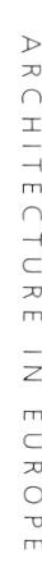

Hampton Court Palace
Detail of the internal façade at the main entrance
Detail der internen Fassade des Haupteingangs
Détail de la façade intérieure de l'entrée principale
Detail van de interne voorgevel van de hoofdingang
1550-1600

◀ **Cambridge**
King's College Chapel
Interior
Innenansicht
Intérieur
Interieur
c. 1446

3

Sculpture in Italy

In the great Italian centres during the Renaissance, particularly Firenze and Roma, the masters (who were often the owners of prosperous workshops) raised sculpture of holy, civic and mythological subjects to the highest levels, working marble, bronze, wood and glazed terracotta. Single statues and groups of sculptures adorn the interiors and exteriors of churches, palaces, squares and gardens, in which the new classical language, so expressive and elegant, sometimes mingled with the late Gothic tradition.

Die Bildhauerei in Italien

In den großen Zentren der Renaissance, es führen Florenz und Rom, bringen die Meister, die fast immer blühende Werkstätten leiten, die Skulptur religiösen, weltlichen, mythologischen Inhalts auf höchstes Niveau und arbeiten mit Marmor, Bronze, Holz und glasierter Terrakotta. Plastiken, einzeln oder als Gruppe, zieren innen und außen religiöse Bauwerke, Paläste, Plätze und Gärten, in denen der neue klassizistische, ausdrucksstarke und elegante Stil zuweilen mit der spätgotischen Tradition verschmilzt.

La sculpture en Italie

Dans les grands centres italiens de la Renaissance, avant tout à Florence et à Rome, les maîtres – souvent à la tête d'ateliers (botteghe) florissants – élèvent la sculpture des sujets sacrés, civils et mythologiques, à de très hauts niveaux en travaillant le marbre, le bronze, le bois et la terre cuite vernissée. Des œuvres plastiques, isolées ou en groupes, viennent orner – à l'intérieur comme à l'extérieur – les édifices religieux, les palais, les places et les jardins où le nouveau langage classique, à la fois expressif et élégant, se marie parfois avec la tradition du gothique tardif.

Beeldhouwkunst in Italië

In de grote Italiaanse centra van de Renaissance, met name in Florence en Rome, brengen de meesters, vaak aan het hoofd van bloeiende werkplaatsen, beeldhouwwerken met religieuze, civiele en mythologische onderwerpen, uitgevoerd in marmer, brons, hout en geglazuurd terracotta, tot grote hoogtes. Sculpturen, losstaand of als groep, decoreren de binnen- en buitenkant van religieuze gebouwen, paleizen, pleinen en tuinen, waarin de nieuwe classicistische, expressieve en elegante stijl versmolten is met de laat-Gotische traditie.

Funeral Monuments
Grabmonumente
Monuments funéraires
Grafmonumenten

Jacopo della Quercia
Tomb of Ilaria del Carretto
Grabmal der Ilaria del Carretto
Monument sépulcral de Ilaria del Carretto
Grafmonument van Ilaria del Carretto
1406-1407
Duomo di San Martino, Lucca

Pietro Lombardo
Monument to doge Pietro Mocenigo
Grabmal des Dogen Pietro Mocenigo
Monument au doge Pietro Mocenigo
Grafmonument voor Pietro Mocenigo
1476
San Zanipolo, Venezia

1400 1420 1440 1460 1480

Antonio Rossellino
Monument to the cardinal of Portogallo
Grabmal des Kardinals von Portugal
Monument au cardinal de Portugal
Grafmonument voor de kardinaal van Portugal
1461-1466
San Miniato al Monte, Firenze

Antonio del Pollaiolo
Tomb of Sixtus IV
Grab Sixtus IV.
Tombeau de Sixte IV
Tombe van Sixtus IV
1484-1493
Basilica di San Pietro, Città del Vaticano

Leone Leoni
Pompeo Leoni
Monument to Carlos V
Grabmal Karl V.
Monument à Charles V
Monument voor Karel V
1550-1600
Monasterio de San Lorenzo, El Escorial

Michelangelo Buonarroti
Tomb of Lorenzo Duke of Urbino
Grab von Lorenzo, Herzog von Urbino
Tombe de Laurent, duc d'Urbino
Tombe van Lorenzo, hertog van Urbino
1524-1531
Cappelle Medicee, San Lorenzo, Firenze

Germain Pilon
Tomb of Jeanne Valentine Balbiani
Grab der Jeanne Valentine Balbiani
Tombeau de Jeanne Valentine Balbiani
Tombe van Jeanne Valentine Balbiani
c. 1573
Musée du Louvre, Paris

1500 1520 1540 1560 1580

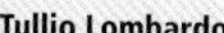

Tullio Lombardo
Funeral Monument of Guidarello Guidarelli
Grabmal des Guidarello Guidarelli
Monument funèbre de Guidarello Guidarelli
Grafmonument voor Guidarello Guidarelli
1525
Galleria dell'Accademia, Ravenna

Michelangelo Buonarroti
Tomb of Julius II
Grab Julius II.
Tombeau de Jules II
Tombe van Julius II
c. 1515
San Pietro in Vincoli, Roma

Lorenzo Ghiberti
(Firenze 1378 - 1455)
Sacrifice of Isaac, bronze
Die Opferung Isaaks, Bronze
Le Sacrifice d'Isaac, bronze
Opoffering van Isaac, brons
1401
45 x 38 cm / 17.7 x 14.9 in.
Museo Nazionale del Bargello, Firenze

Filippo Brunelleschi
(Firenze 1377 - 1446)
Sacrifice of Isaac, bronze
Die Opferung Isaaks, Bronze
Le Sacrifice d'Isaac, bronze
Opoffering van Isaac, brons
1401
45 x 38 cm / 17.7 x 14.9 in.
Museo Nazionale del Bargello, Firenze

Lorenzo Ghiberti
(Firenze 1378 - 1455)
North Doors, the *Crucifixion* panel, bronze
Nordtür, Panel mit der *Kreuzigung*, Bronze
Porte Nord, détail de la *La Crucifixion*, bronze
Noordelijke deur, paneel met de *Kruisiging*, brons
52 x 45 cm / 20.4 x 17.7 in.
1403-1424
Battistero, Firenze

Lorenzo Ghiberti
(Firenze 1378 - 1455)
Gates of Paradise, detail of the *Meeting of King Solomon and the Queen of Sheba*, bronze
Die Paradiestür, Detail mit dem *Treffen zwischen Salomon und der Königin von Saba*, Bronze
Porte orientale du baptistère, dite « *du Paradis* », détail avec *La Rencontre de Salomon et de la reine de Saba*, bronze
Paradijspoort, detail met de ontmoeting tussen *Salomon en de koningin van Sheba*, brons
1425-1452
80 x 79 cm / 31.4 x 31.1 in.
Museo dell'Opera del Duomo, Firenze

"Jacopo, with Ilaria, sculpted Italy lost in death when its age was purer and essential."
"Jacopo meißelte mit Ilaria das im Tode verlorene Italien als sein Alter rein und bedeutungsvoll war."
« Avec Ilaria, Jacopo sculpta l'Italie perdue dans la mort, quand l'époque était plus pure et plus exigeante. »
"Jacopo houwde met Ilaria Italië, verloren in de dood toen haar leeftijd op haar puurst en noodzakelijkst was."
Pier Paolo Pasolini

Jacopo della Quercia
(Querciagrossa, Siena c. 1371 - Siena 1438)
Tomb of Ilaria del Carretto, marble
Grabmal der Ilaria del Carretto, Marmor
Tombeau d'Ilaria del Carretto, marbre
Grafmonument van Ilaria del Carretto, marmer
244 x 88 x 66,5 cm / 96 x 34.6 x 26.2 in.
1406-1407
Duomo di San Martino, Lucca

Donatello
(Firenze 1386 - 1466)
David
Bronze
Brons
c. 1440
h. 158 cm / 62.2 in.
Museo Nazionale del Bargello, Firenze

CAMPO
DI S.S. GIOVANNI
E PAOLO

Donatello
(Firenze 1386 - 1466)
Judith and Holofernes, bronze
Judith und Holofernes, Bronze
Judith et Holopherne, bronze
Judith en Holofernes, brons
1455-1460
h. 236 cm / 92.9 in.
Palazzo Vecchio, Firenze

◀ **Andrea del Verrocchio**
(Firenze 1435 - Venezia 1488)
Equestrian monument to Bartolomeo Colleoni, bronze
Reitermonument von Bartolomeo Colleoni, Bronze
Statue équestre de Bartolomeo Colleoni, bronze
Ruiterstandbeeld van Bartolomeo Colleoni, brons
1479-1488
h. 395 cm / 155.5 in.
Campo Santi Giovanni e Paolo, Venezia

Donatello
Choir-stall, marble
Sängerkanzel, Marmor
Tribune des chantres, marbre
Koortribune, marmer
1433-1439
210 x 507 cm / 82.6 x 199.6 in.
Museo dell'Opera del Duomo, Firenze

Luca della Robbia
(Firenze c. 1400 - 1482)
Choir-stall, detail of youthful singers, marble
Sängerkanzel, Detail mit singenden Knaben, Marmor
Jeunes chantres, détail de la *Tribune des chantres*, marbre
Koortribune, detail met jonge koorzangers, marmer
1431-1439
104 x 64 cm / 40.9 x 25.2
Museo dell'Opera del Duomo, Firenze

Luca della Robbia
(Firenze c. 1400 - 1482)
Visitation, glazed terracotta
Heimsuchung, glasierte Terrakotta
La Visitation, terre cuite vernissée
Visitatie, geglazuurd terracota
c. 1445
h. 155 cm / 61 in.
San Giovanni Fuorcivitas, Pistoia

► **Luca della Robbia**
(Firenze c. 1400 - 1482)
Tondo with Virgin and Child, glazed terracotta
Tondo mit Madonna und Kind, glasierte Terrakotta
Vierge à l'Enfant, terre cuite vernissée
Tondo met Madonna en Kind, geglazuurd terracotta
1475-1480
ø 100 cm / 39.3 in.
Museo Nazionale del Bargello, Firenze

Andrea del Verrocchio
(Firenze 1435 - Venezia 1488)
David
Bronze
Brons
c. 1466
h. 120 cm / 47.2 in.
Museo Nazionale del Bargello,
Firenze

▶ **Antonio del Pollaiolo**
(Firenze c. 1431 - Roma 1498)
Hercules and Antaeus, bronze
Herkules und Antäus, Bronze
Hercule et Antée, bronze
Herakles en Antaios, brons
c. 1475
h. 45 cm / 17.7 in.
Museo Nazionale del Bargello,
Firenze

"[Michelangelo] In the statues he was clearly more proficient than any other modern man who had worked until then."
"Was die Skulpturen anbelangt, bewies er [Michelangelo] außerordentlich zu sein, mehr als jeder andere Zeitgenosse, der bis dahin gearbeitet hatte."
« [Michelangelo] Il montra dans les statues qu'il excellait plus que tout autre de ses contemporains qui eût travaillé jusque-là. »
"[Michelangelo] Wat betreft de beelden, bewees hij voortreffelijker te zijn dan al zijn andere tijdgenoten, die tot dan toe hadden gewerkt."
Giorgio Vasari

Michelangelo Buonarroti
(Caprese, Arezzo 1475 - Roma 1564)
Battle of the Centaurs, marble
Schlacht zwischen den Zentauren und den Lapithen, Marmor
Le Combat des Centaures et des Lapithes, marbre
Strijd tussen Centaurs en Lapithen, marmer
c. 1492
84,5 x 90,5 cm / 33.2 x 35.6 in.
Casa Buonarroti, Firenze

▶ **Antonio Rossellino**
(Settignano, Firenze 1427 - Firenze 1478/1481)
Madonna del Latte (Madonna of the Milk), detail
Madonna del Latte, Detail
La Madone au lait, détail
Zogende Madonna, detail
1478
320 x 160 cm / 125.9 x 62.9 in.
Santa Croce, Firenze

Michelangelo Buonarroti
(Caprese, Arezzo 1475 - Roma 1564)
Bacco / Bacchus
Marble
Marmor
Marbre
Marmer
1496-1497
h. 184 cm / 72.4 in
Museo Nazionale del Bargello, Firenze

◀ **Michelangelo Buonarroti**
(Caprese, Arezzo 1475 - Roma 1564)
Pietà
Marble
Marmor
Marbre
Marmer
1498-1499
h. 174 cm / 68.5 in.
Basilica di San Pietro, Città del Vaticano

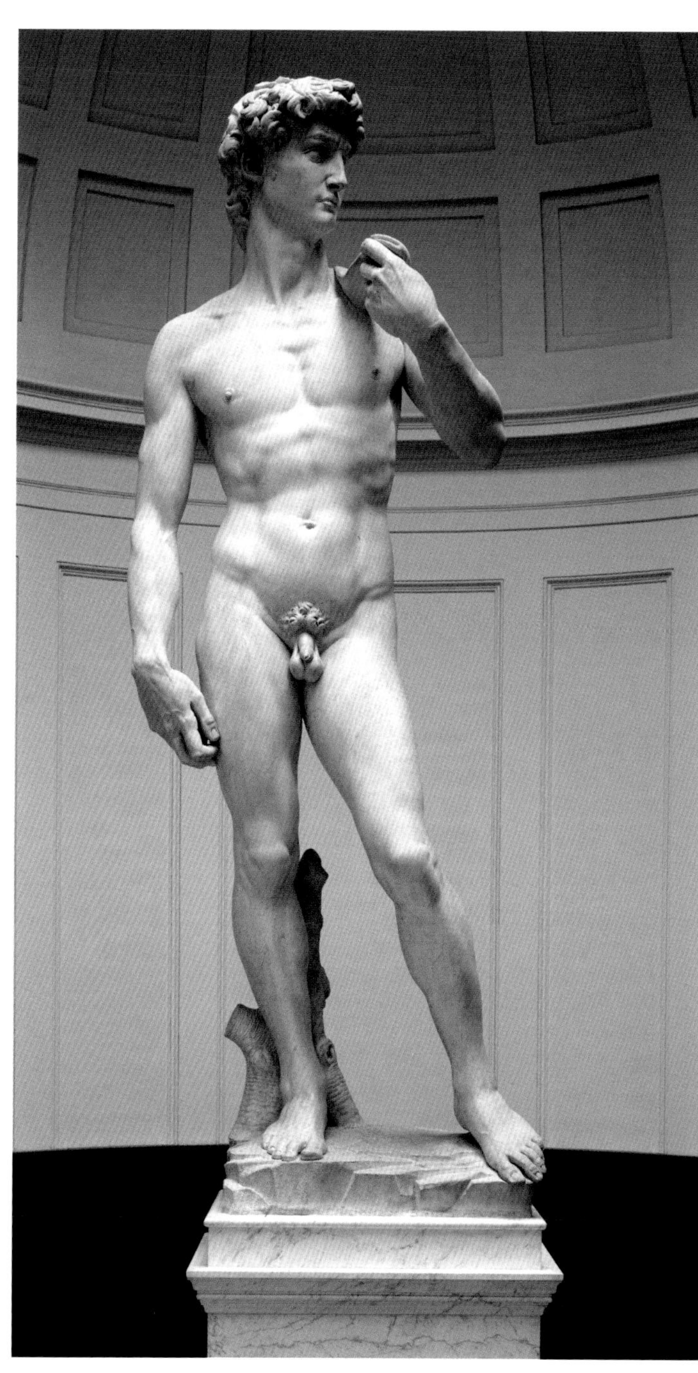

Michelangelo Buonarroti
(Caprese, Arezzo 1475 - Roma 1564)
David
Marble
Marmor
Marbre
Marmer
1501-1504
h. 410 cm / 161.4 in.
Galleria dell'Accademia, Firenze

▶ **Michelangelo Buonarroti**
(Caprese, Arezzo 1475 - Roma 1564)
Madonna and Child with St. John, known as the *Tondo Pitti*, marble
Madonna mit Kind und Johannes der Täufer, genannt *Tondo Pitti*, Marmor
La Vierge à l'Enfant avec saint Jean-Baptiste enfant (Tondo Pitti), marbre
Madonna met het Kind en de kleine Sint Johannes, beter bekend als *Tondo Pitti*, marmer
c. 1503
85,5 x 82 cm / 33.6 x 32.2 in.
Museo Nazionale del Bargello, Firenze

Michelangelo Buonarroti
(Caprese, Arezzo 1475 - Roma 1564)
Dying Slave, marble
Sterbender Sklave, Marmor
Esclave mourant, marbre
Stervende slaaf, marmer
1513-1515
h. 228 cm / 89.7 in.
Musée du Louvre, Paris

Michelangelo Buonarroti
(Caprese, Arezzo 1475 - Roma 1564)
Rebellious Slave, marble
Rebellierender Sklave, Marmor
Esclave rebelle, marbre
Rebelse slaaf, marmer
1513-1515
h. 228 cm / 89.7 in.
Musée du Louvre, Paris

▶ **Michelangelo Buonarroti**
(Caprese, Arezzo 1475 - Roma 1564)
Tomb of Julius II, detail of Moses, marble
Grab von Julius II, Detail mit Moses, Marmor
Tombeau de Jules II, détail avec le *Moïse*, marbre
Tombe van Julius II, detail met Mozes, marmer
c. 1515
h. 215 cm / 84.6 in.
San Pietro in Vincoli, Roma

Michelangelo Buonarroti
(Caprese, Arezzo 1475 - Roma 1564)
Tomb of Lorenzo Duke of Urbino, marble
Grab von Lorenzo, Herzog von Urbino, Marmor
Tombeau de Laurent de Médicis, duc d'Urbino, marbre
Tombe van Lorenzo, hertog van Urbino, Marmer
1524-1531
Cappelle Medicee, San Lorenzo, Firenze

"An excellent artist has no idea | that the marble alone does not surround | with its mass, and that the discovery depends only | on the hand guided by the intellect."

„Der größte Künstler hat keinerlei Vorstellung, / die nicht bereits vom Marmor umschrieben ist / und so erreicht er sie nur, / wenn die Hand dem Geiste gehorcht."

« Le meilleur artiste n'a aucun concept/qu'un marbre seul en lui ne circonscrive/avec son excès ; à cela seul arrive/la main qui suit l'ordre de l'intellect ».

"De grootste kunstenaar heeft geen enkel concept / dat niet al in het marmer is omvat / en dit kan alleen bereikt worden met / een hand die gehoorzaam is aan het verstand."

Michelangelo Buonarroti

Michelangelo Buonarroti
(Caprese, Arezzo 1475 - Roma 1564)
Pietà Rondinini
Marble
Marmor
Marbre
Marmer
1552-1564
h. 195 cm / 76.7 in.
Castello Sforzesco, Milano

Jacopo Sansovino
(Firenze 1486 - Venezia 1570)
Miracle of the Soldier in Lombardy, bronze
Das Wunder der Soldaten in der Lombardei, Bronze
Le Miracle du soldat en Lombardie, bronze
Het wonder van de soldaat in Lombardije, brons
1541-1546
San Marco, Venezia

◀ **Jacopo Sansovino**
(Firenze 1486 - Venezia 1570)
Bacchus and a Young Faun, marble
Bacchus und Faun, Marmor
Bacchus et un faune, marbre
Bacchus en een faun, marmer
1512-1515
h. 146 cm / 57.4 in.
Museo Nazionale del Bargello, Firenze

◀ **Benvenuto Cellini**
(Firenze 1500 - 1571)
Perseus, bronze
Perseus, Bronze
Persée, bronze
Perseus, brons
1545-1554
h. 320 cm / 125.9 in.
Loggia dei Lanzi, Firenze

Benvenuto Cellini
(Firenze 1500 - 1571)
Bust of Cosimo I, bronze
Büste des Cosimos I, Bronze
Buste de Côme Ier, bronze
Buste van Cosimo I, brons
1546-1547
h. 110 cm / 43.3 in.
Museo Nazionale del Bargello, Firenze

Giambologna
(Douai 1529 - Firenze 1608)
Rape of the Sabines, marble
Raub der Sabinerinnen, Marmor
L'Enlèvement des Sabines, marbre
De Sabbijnse Maagdenroof, marmer
1582
h. 410 cm / 161.4 in.
Loggia dei Lanzi, Firenze

◀ **Giambologna**
(Douai 1529 - Firenze 1608)
Fountain of Neptune, detail, bronze and marble
Neptunsbrunnen, Detail, Bronze und Marmor
Fontaine de Neptune, détail, bronze et marbre
Fontein van Neptunus, detail, brons en marmer
1563-1566
h. 91,4 cm / 35.9 in.
Piazza del Nettuno, Bologna

Agostino di Duccio
(Firenze 1418 - Perugia c. 1481)
Cappella di Isotta
Details with musician angels
Detail mit musizierenden Engeln
Détail des Anges musiciens
Detail met musicerende engelen
1449-1455
Tempio Malatestiano, Rimini

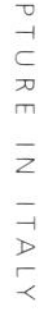

Francesco Laurana
(La Vrana, Zara c. 1430 - Avignon 1502)
Eleonora d'Aragona, bust, marble
Büste der Eleonore von Aragon, Marmor
Buste d'Éléonore d'Aragon, marbre
Buste van Eleonora d'Aragona, marmer
c. 1450
h. 50 cm / 19.6 in.
Galleria Nazionale della Sicilia, Palermo

Guido Mazzoni
(Modena c. 1450 - 1518)
Madonna della pappa, glazed terracotta
Breimadonna, Terrakotta mehrfarbig
La Madone à la bouillie, terre cuite polychrome
Madonna met de pap, polychroom terracotta
1480
Duomo, Modena

◀ **Bartolomé Ordoñez**
(Burgos c. 1490 - Carrara 1520)
Altar, detail of the *Epiphany*, marble
Altar, Detail mit der *Epiphanie*, Marmor
L'Épiphanie, détail du *Retable*, marbre
Altaar, detail met het feest van *Epifanie*, marmer
c. 1516
San Giovanni a Carbonara, Napoli

Guido Mazzoni
(Modena c. 1450 - 1518)
Lamentation over the Dead Christ, detail of Mary Magdalene, glazed terracotta
Beweinung Christi, Detail mit der Maria Magdalena, Terracotta mehrfarbig
Marie-Madeleine, détail de *La Déploration du Christ*, terre cuite polychrome
Bewening van de dode Christus, detail met Maria Magdalena, polychroom terracotta
1492
Sant'Anna dei Lombardi, Napoli

▶ **Niccolò dell'Arca**
(Bari c. 1435/1440 - Bologna 1494)
Mourning of the Marias over the Dead Christ, detail, terracotta with traces of colour
Die Beweinung Christi, Detail, Terrakotta mit Farbspuren
La Déploration du Christ, détail, terre cuite avec traces de polychromie
Bewening van de dode Christus, detail, terracotta met sporen van polychromie
c. 1485
Santa Maria della Vita, Bologna

Sculpture in Europe

In France, Spain, Austria and Germany, sculpture progressively absorbed the new expressive means of the Renaissance that radiated out from Italy, and united them with the late Gothic style and local traditions. Artists such as Goujon, Berruguete and Pacher succeeded in renewing monumental sculpture and ornamentation in the light of the new sculptural languages with works that were at times dramatic, at times refined and elegant, with subjects that ranged from mythology to sacred themes.

Bildhauerei in Europa

In Frankreich, Spanien, Österreich und Deutschland begegnet die Bildhauerei allmählich den neuen Ausdrucksmitteln der Renaissance, die von Italien ausgehen, und verbindet sie mit Modellen, die an die Spätgotik sowie an lokale Traditionen gebunden sind. Künstler wie Goujon, Berruguete und Pacher beginnen im Licht der modernen Stilformen die Statuen, Monumente oder Dekoration, mit einem jetzt dramatischen, jetzt raffinierten und eleganten Ton zu erneuern, wobei die Themen von mythologischen bis hin zu religiösen Inhalten reichen.

4

La sculpture en Europe

En France comme en Espagne, en Autriche comme en Allemagne, la sculpture aborde progressivement les nouveaux moyens d'expression nés de la Renaissance italienne, qu'elle fusionne avec les modèles hérités du gothique tardif et des traditions locales. À la lumière de ces langages plus modernes, des artistes comme Goujon, Berruguete et Pacher arrivent à renouveler la statuaire monumentale ou ornementale avec des œuvres de tonalité tantôt spectaculaire, tantôt élégante et raffinée, qui vont des sujets mythologiques aux thèmes sacrés.

Beeldhouwkunst in Europa

De beeldhouwkunst ontmoet in Frankrijk, Spanje, Oostenrijk en Duitsland geleidelijk aan de uit Italië overgewaaide nieuwe renaissancistische expressieve middelen en versmelt dit met de modellen die verbonden zijn aan de laat-Gotische en lokale tradities. Kunstenaars als Goujon, Berreguete en Pacher beginnen, met het oog op de nieuwste stijlen, met het vernieuwen van de monumentale beeldhouwwerken of van de ornamentatie, met werken van soms dramatische, dan weer verfijnde en elegante aard, die variëren van mythologische tot religieuze thema's.

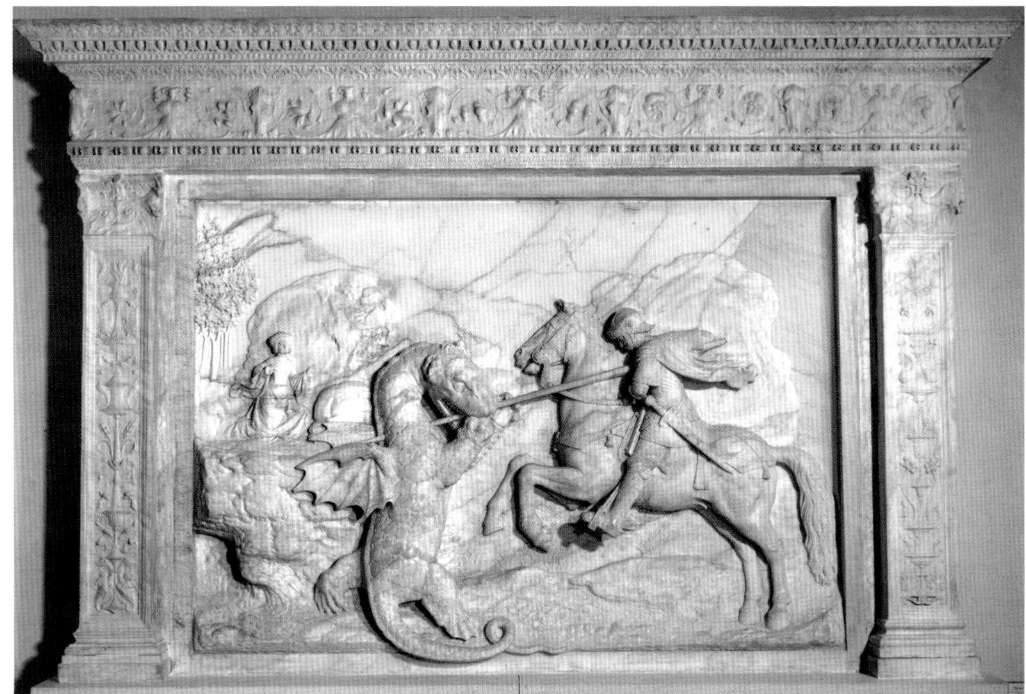

Michel Colombe
(Bourges c. 1430 - Tours 1512)
Saint George and the Dragon, marble
Der Heilige Georg und der Drache, Marmor
Saint Georges combattant le dragon, marbre
Sint Joris en de draak, marmer
1509-1510
128 x 182 cm / 50.3 x 71.6 in.
Musée du Louvre, Paris

▶ **Pierre Bontemps**
(Sens c. 1507 - Verneuil-sur-Oise 1568)
Claude de France in Prayer, marble
Betende Statue von Claude de France, Marmor
Claude de France en orante, marbre
Beeld van de biddende Claude de France, marmer
1549-1559
Basilique, Saint-Denis

Jean Goujon
(*c.* 1510 - Bologna *c.* 1566)
Nymph and Cupid
Nymphe und Genius
Nymphe et Génie
Nimf en Geest
1547-1549
Musée du Louvre, Paris

Germain Pilon
(Paris 1528 - 1590)
Tomb of Jeanne Valentine Balbiani, detail, marble
Grabmal der Jeanne Valentine Balbiani, Detail, Marmor
Tombeau de Valentine Balbiani, détail, marbre
Tombe van Jeanne Valentine Balbiani, detail, marmer
c. 1573
83 x 191 cm / 32.6 x 75.2 in.
Musée du Louvre, Paris

◀ **Germain Pilon**
(Paris 1528 - 1590)
Mourning Virgin, glazed terracotta
Die leidende Jungfrau, Terrakotta mehrfarbig
Vierge de douleur, terre cuite polychrome
Onze-Lieve-Vrouw van Smarten, polychroom terracotta
1550-1600
h. 159 cm / 62.5 in.
Musée du Louvre, Paris

Alonso Berruguete
(Paredes de Nava c. 1486 - Toledo 1561)
Saint Christopher, wood with polychromy
Heiliger Christophorus, Holz mehrfarbig
Saint Christophe, bois polychromé
Sint Christoffel, hout met polychromie
1534
Museo Nacional de Escultura, Valladolid

Juan de Juni
(Borgogna 1506 - Valladolid 1577)
Burial of Christ, detail, wood with polychromy
Grablegung Christi, Detail, Holz mehrfarbig
La Mise au tombeau, détail, bois polychrome
De begrafenis van Christus, detail, hout met polychromie
1541-1545
Museo Nacional de Escultura, Valladolid

Michael Pacher
(Brunico, Bolzano c. 1435 - Salzburg 1498)
Crowning of the Virgin, detail, wood with polychromy
Die Krönung der Jungfrau, Detail, Holz mehrfarbig
Le Couronnement de la Vierge, détail, bois polychrome
Kroning van de Maagd, detail, hout met polychromie
1479-1481
Pfarramt St. Wolfgang, St. Wolfgang im Salzkammergut

Adam Kraf
(Nürnberg 1455/1460 - 1508/1509)
A Station of the Cross, terracotta with traces of colour
Kreuzwegstation, Terrakotta mit Farbspuren
Station du Chemin de croix, terre cuite avec traces de polychromie
Statie van de Kruisweg, terracotta met sporen van polychromie
1490
Johannisfriedhof, Nürnberg

Veit Stoss
(Horb, Schwaben 1437/1447
- Nürnberg 1533)
Group of Apostles, marble
Apostelgruppe, Marmor
Apôtres, marbre
Groep van Apostelen, marmer
c. 1500-1530
Diözesanmuseum, Bamberg

Étienne Bobillet
Paul de Mosselman
Mourners, alabaster
Trauerde Figuren, Alabaster
Pleurants, albâtre
Figuren in rouw, albast
c. 1453
h. 38,7 cm / 15.2 in.
Metropolitan Museum of Art, New York

▶ **Tilman Riemenschneider**
(Osterode c. 1460 - Würzburg 1531)
Tomb of Emperor Henry II and his wife Cunegond, detail of a female figure
Grab vom Kaiser Heinrich II und seiner Ehefrau Kunigunde, Detail mit weiblicher Figur
Tombeau de l'empereur Henri II et de sa femme Cunégonde, détail
Tombe van Keizer Hendrik II en zijn vrouw Cunegonda, detail met vrouwelijk figuur
1499-1513
Dom, Bamberg

Nikolaus Gerhaert von Leyden
(Leiden c. 1430 - Wien 1473)
The Thinker, sandstone
Der Denker, Sandstein
Buste d'homme accoudé, grès rose
Denkend figuur, zandsteen
c. 1450
44 x 32 x 31 cm / 17.3 x 12.5 x 12.2 in.
Musée de l'Oeuvre Notre-Dame, Strasburg

▶ **Konrad Meit**
(Worms c. 1480 - Antwerpen 1550/1551)
Mars and Venus, bronze
Mars und Venus, Bronze
Mars et Vénus, bronze
Mars en Venus, brons
1520
Germanisches Nationalmuseum, Nürnberg

Painting in Central and Southern Italy

Italian Renaissance painting, which produced its first great results in Firenze, soon reached Roma and other cities through the works of artists such as Masaccio, Piero della Francesca, Leonardo and Michelangelo. These great masters of unsurpassed masterpieces, who represented a multifaceted artistic culture, enriched the churches and palaces with their paintings commissioned by nobles, religious orders and popes. Perspective, naturalism, classicism, studies of nature and anatomy, all constituted the fundamental elements of their compositions and their pursuit of their art.

Die Malerei in Mittel- und Süditalien

Die italienische Malerei der Renaissance, deren erste bedeutende Ergebnisse man in Florenz verzeichnet, breitet sich nach Rom und in andere Zentren aus, mit Künstlern wie Masaccio, Piero della Francesca, Leonardo und Michelangelo. Diese Meister großer, unübertroffener Kunstwerke sind Vertreter einer polyvalenten künstlerischen Kultur und haben mit ihren Malereien Kirchen und Paläste auf Auftrag von Herren, religiösen Orden und Päpsten geschmückt. Die Perspektive, der Naturalismus, der Klassizismus, das Erforschen der Natur, das Studium der Anatomie, das sind die grundlegenden Elemente dieser malerischen Studien.

5

La peinture dans l'Italie du Centre et du Sud

La peinture italienne de la Renaissance – dont les premières réalisations se font à Florence et en Toscane – se propage ensuite vers Rome et les autres centres, avec des artistes comme Masaccio, Piero della Francesca, Léonard de Vinci et Michel-Ange. Ces créateurs de chefs-d'œuvre insurpassés, représentants d'une culture artistique polyvalente et protéiforme, ont enrichi églises et palais d'une foule de tableaux commandités par des nobles, des ordres religieux et des papes. La perspective, le naturalisme, le classicisme, l'exploration de la nature et l'étude de l'anatomie constituent les éléments fondamentaux de la recherche picturale.

Schilderkunst in Midden en Zuid-Italië

De Italiaanse schilderkunst van de Renaissance, waarmee de eerste grote resultaten werden geboekt in Florence, verspreidde zich richting Rome en andere centra met dank aan kunstenaars als Masaccio, Piero della Francesca, Leonardo en Michelangelo. Deze meesters van onovertroffen meesterwerken, vertegenwoordigers van een veelzijdige artistieke cultuur, hebben in opdracht van edelen, religieuze orders en pausen, kerken en paleizen verrijkt met hun schilderingen. Het perspectief, het naturalisme, het classicisme, het onderzoeken van de natuur en het bestuderen van de anatomie, vertegenwoordigen de fundamentele samenstellende elementen voor de studie van het schilderen.

Portraiture
Das Portrait
Le portrait
Het portret

Hans Memling
Portrait of a Man with a Letter
Portrait eines Mannes mit Brief
Portrait de l'homme à la lettre
Portret van een man
c. 1490
Galleria degli Uffizi, Firenze

Antonello da Messina
Portrait
Portret
1465-1470
Museo Mandralisca, Cefalù

Petrus Christus
Portrait of a Young Girl
Portrait eines Mädchens
Portrait de jeune femme
Portret van een jong edelvrouw
c. 1470
Gemäldegalerie, Staatliche Museen, Berlin

1420 1440 1460 1480 1500 15

Donatello
Niccolò da Uzzano
c. 1430-1432
Museo del Bargello, Firenze

Francesco Laurana
Bust of Eleonora d'Aragona
Büste der Eleonore von Aragon
Buste d'Éléonore d'Aragon
Buste van Eleonora d'Aragona
c. 1450
Galleria Nazionale della Sicilia, Palermo

Mino da Fiesole
Piero de' Medici
1453
Museo Nazionale del Bargello, Firenze

Albrecht Dürer
Portrait of Oswolt Krel
Bildnis des Oswald Krel
Portrait d'Oswald Krel
Portret van Oswolt Krel
1499
Alte Pinakothek, München

Giovanni Bellini
Portrait of a Young Man
Portrait eines Mannes
Portrait d'homme
Portret van een man
c. 1500
Galleria degli Uffizi, Firenze

Agnolo Bronzino
Portrait of Lucrezia Pucci Panciatichi
Portrait der Lucrezia Pucci Panciatichi
Portrait de Lucrezia Pucci Panciatichi
Portret van Lucretia Pucci Panciatichi
c. 1540
Galleria degli Uffizi, Firenze

1540 1542 1542 1544 1546

Desiderio da Settignano
Bust of a Lady
Büste einer Edelfrau
Buste de jeune femme
Buste van een Edelvrouw
c. 1455-1460
Museo Nazionale del Bargello, Firenze

Andrea del Verrocchio
Lady with a Nosegay
Die Dame mit dem Sträußchen
Dame au bouquet
Dame met bloemen
c. 1475
Museo Nazionale del Bargello, Firenze

Benvenuto Cellini
Bust of Cosimo I
Büste des Cosimo I.
Buste de Côme Ier
Buste van Cosimo I
1546-1547
Museo Nazionale del Bargello, Firenze

Masaccio
(San Giovanni Valdarno, Arezzo 1401 - Roma 1428)
Expulsion from Paradise, fresco
Vertreibung aus dem Paradies, Fresko
Adam et Ève chassés du paradis, fresque
Verdreven uit het Paradijs, fresco
1424-1426
208 x 88 cm / 81.8 x 34.6 in.
Santa Maria del Carmine, Firenze

► **Masaccio**
(San Giovanni Valdarno, Arezzo 1401 - Roma 1428)
Trinity, fresco
Trinität, Fresko
La Trinité, fresque
Drie-eenheid, fresco
1426-1428
667 x 317 cm / 262.6 x 124 in.
Santa Maria Novella, Firenze

Gentile da Fabriano
(Fabriano c. 1370 - Roma 1427)
Adoration of the Magi, tempera on wood and tooled gold leaf
Anbetung der Heiligen Drei Könige, Tempera auf Holzplatte und Blattgold
L'Adoration des Mages, détrempe sur bois
Aanbidding der Wijzen, tempera op paneel en bladgoud
1423
301,5 x 283 cm / 118.7 x 111.4 in
Galleria degli Uffizi, Firenze

Beato Angelico
(Vicchio, Firenze c. 1395 - Roma 1455)
Cortona Altarpiece with the Annunciation, tempera on wood
Altarbild der Verkündigung von Cortona, Tempera auf Holz
Retable de Cortona avec *l'Annonciation*, détrempe sur bois
Altaarstuk van Cortona met de Annunciatie, tempera op paneel
1433-1434
175 x 180 cm / 68.8 x 70.8 in.
Museo Diocesano, Cortona

Paolo Uccello
(Pratovecchio, Arezzo 1397 - Firenze 1475)
The Battle of San Romano: Dishorsing of Bernardino della Ciarda, tempera on wood
Die Schlacht von San Romano: Der Sieg über Bernardino della Ciarda, Tempera auf Holz
La Bataille de San Romano : Bernardino della Ciarda désarçonné, détrempe sur bois
De Slag bij San Romano: Bernardino della Ciarda van zijn paard geworpen, tempera op paneel
c. 1438
188 x 327 cm / 74 x 128.7 in.
Galleria degli Uffizi, Firenze

- *"Oh what a sweet thing this perspective is!"*
- *"Ach wie süß ist diese Perspektive!"*
- *«Oh, quelle douce chose est cette perspective!»*
- *"Oh hoe zoet is dit perspectief!"*

Paolo Uccello

Piero della Francesca
(Borgo San Sepolcro, Arezzo 1415/1420 - 1492)
Flagellation, tempera and oil on wood
Die Geißelung Christi, Tempera und Öl auf Holz
La Flagellation, détrempe et huile sur bois
De Geseling, tempera en olieverf op paneel
c. 1455
59 x 81,5 cm / 23.2 x 32 in.
Galleria Nazionale delle Marche Urbino

▶ **Piero della Francesca**
(Borgo San Sepolcro, Arezzo 1415/1420 - 1492)
Madonna del Parto, fresco
Madonna der Geburt, Fresko
La Madonna del Parto, fresque
Maria in Verwachting, fresco
c. 1460
260 x 203 cm / 102.3 x 79.9 in
Museo della Madonna del Parto, Monterchi, Arezzo

Piero della Francesca
(Borgo San Sepolcro, Arezzo 1415/1420 - 1492)
History of the True Cross: Battle of Heraclius and Khosrau, fresco
Die Geschichte vom Kreuzes: Die Schlacht zwischen Heraklius und Chosroes, Fresko
La Légende de la Vraie Croix : la victoire d'Héraclius sur Chosroès, fresque
Legende van het Ware Kruis: Strijd tussen Heraclius en Khusro, fresco
c. 1460
329 x 747 cm / 129.5 x 294 in
San Francesco, Arezzo

▶ **Piero della Francesca**
(Borgo San Sepolcro, Arezzo 1415/1420 - 1492)
Portraits of Federico da Montefeltro and Battista Sforza, dukes of Urbino, tempera on wood
Diptychon des Federico da Montefeltro mi seiner Gattin Battista Sforza, Herzöge von Urbino, Tempera auf Holz
Portraits de Federico da Montefeltro et de Battista Sforza, duc et duchesse d'Urbino, détrempe sur bois
Portret van Federico da Montefeltro en Battista Sforza, hertogin van Urbino, tempera op paneel
c. 1465
47 x 33 cm / 18.5 x 12.9 in
Galleria degli Uffizi, Firenze

Benozzo Gozzoli
(Firenze 1420 - Pistoia 1497)
Procession of the Magi, east wall, fresco
Der Zug der Heiligen Drei Könige, Ostwand, Fresko
Le Cortège des Mages, mur Est, fresque
De optocht der Drie Koningen, oostwand, fresco
1459-1460
76 x 96 cm / 29.9 x 37.7 in.
Palazzo Medici Riccardi, Firenze

◀ **Piero della Francesca**
(San Sepolcro, Arezzo 1415/1420 - 1492)
Brera Altarpiece (or Madonna and Child with Saints and Duke of Urbino), oil on wood
Madonna mit Kind und Heiligen und dem Stifter Federico da Montefeltro (auch Pala di Brera), Öl auf Holz
Sainte Conversation (Retable de Brera), huile sur bois
Madonna met Hertog Federico (of altaarstuk van Brera), olieverf op paneel
1472-1474
248 x 170 cm / 97.6 x 66.9 in.
Pinacoteca di Brera, Milano

◀ **Filippo Lippi**
(Firenze c. 1406 - Spoleto 1469)
Madonna and Child with Two Angels, tempera on wood
Madonna mit Kind und Engeln, Tempera auf Holz
Vierge à l'Enfant et deux anges, détrempe sur bois
Madonna met het Kind en Engelen, tempera op paneel
1460-1465
95 x 62 cm / 37.4 x 24.4 in.
Galleria degli Uffizi, Firenze

Antonio del Pollaiolo
(Firenze c. 1431 - Roma 1498)
Portrait of a Young Girl, oil on wood
Bildnis eines Mädchens, Öl auf Holz
Portrait d'une jeune femme, huile sur bois
Portret van een meisje, olieverf op paneel
c. 1465
52,5 x 36,5 cm / 20.7 x 14.8 in.
Gemäldegalerie, Staatliche Museen, Berlin

Sandro Botticelli
(Firenze 1445 - 1510)
Madonna of the Magnificat, tempera on wood
Madonna des Magnificat, Tempera auf Holz
La Madone du Magnificat, détrempe sur bois
Madonna van het Magnificat, tempera op paneel
1480-1489
ø 118 cm / 46.4 in.
Galleria degli Uffizi, Firenze

Sandro Botticelli
(Firenze 1445 - 1510)
Madonna of the Pomegranate, tempera on wood
Madonna mit dem Granatapfel, Tempera auf Holz
La Madone à la grenade, détrempe sur bois
Madonna met de Granaatappel, tempera op paneel
1487
ø 143,5 cm / 56.4 in.
Galleria degli Uffizi, Firenze

"Sandro [Botticelli] drew so well without mannerism and so much that for a long time those who came after him used all of their wits to possess some of his drawings."
"Sandro [Botticelli] malte anders als gewöhnlich und so versuchten noch lange nach ihm die Künstler seine Bilder zu haben."
«Sandro [Botticelli] dessinait d'une façon plus que merveilleuse, au point qu'après lui, beaucoup d'artistes s'efforcèrent d'avoir de ses dessins.»
"Sandro [Botticelli] schilderde zo ongewoon goed, dat na hem kunstenaars zich inspanden om zijn ontwerpen te bemachtigen."
Giorgio Vasari

Sandro Botticelli
(Firenze 1445 - 1510)
Spring, tempera on wood
Frühling, Tempera auf Holz
Le Printemps, détrempe sur bois
De Lente, tempera op paneel
1482-1485
207 x 319 cm / 81.4 x 125.5 in
Galleria degli Uffizi, Firenze

Sandro Botticelli
(Firenze 1445 - 1510)
Birth of Venus, tempera on canvas
Die Geburt der Venus, Tempera auf Leinwand
La Naissance de Vénus, détrempe sur toile
Geboorte van Venus, tempera op doek
1484-1485
172,5 x 278,5 cm / 67.9 x 109.6 in.
Galleria degli Uffizi, Firenze

Perugino
(Città della Pieve, Perugia c. 1450 - Fontignano, Perugia 1523)
Christ Giving the Keys to Saint Peter, fresco
Christus übergibt Petrus die Schlüssel, Fresko
La Remise des clés à saint Pierre, fresque
De overhandiging van de sleutel aan Petrus, fresco
1481-1482
Cappella Sistina, Palazzi Vaticani, Città del Vaticano

Leonardo da Vinci
(Firenze 1445 - 1510)
Annunciation, tempera on wood
Verkündigung, Tempera auf Holz
L'Annonciation, détrempe sur bois
Annunciatie, tempera op paneel
1489-1490
150 x 156 cm / 59 x 61.4 in.
Galleria degli Uffizi, Firenze

"Painting is poetry to be seen and not heard, poetry is painting to be heard and not seen. Now it follows that these two poetries or two paintings, as you wish, have exchanged the senses they use to penetrate the intellect."

"Die Malerei ist eine Poesie, die man sieht und nicht hört, und die Poesie ist eine Malerei, die man hört und nicht sieht. So haben diese beiden Poesien, oder wenn du willst, die zwei Malereien, die Sinne vertauscht, mit denen sie in den Geist eindringen sollten."

«La peinture est une poésie que l'on voit sans l'entendre, et la poésie est une peinture que l'on entend sans la voir. Ces deux poésies – ou dira-t-on ces deux peintures – ont échangé les sens par lesquels elles devraient accéder à l'intellect.»

"Een schilderij is poëzie die men ziet maar niet voelt en poëzie is een schilderij dat men voelt, maar niet ziet. Zo hebben deze twee poëziën, of als u wilt, schilderijen de gevoelens verwisseld, waarvoor zij het verstand hebben moeten doordringen."
Leonardo da Vinci

Leonardo da Vinci
(Vinci, Firenze 1452 - Amboise 1519)
Virgin of the Rocks, oil on wood, transposed to canvas
Die Jungfrau der Felsen, Öl auf Holz, auf Leinwand übertragen
La Vierge aux rochers, huile sur bois, transposée sur toile
De Maagd op de rotsen, olieverf op paneel, overgebracht op doek
1483-1486
199 x 122 cm / 78.3 x 48 in.
Musée du Louvre, Paris

Leonardo da Vinci
(Vinci, Firenze 1452 - Amboise 1519)
Virgin and Child with Saint Anne, oil on wood
Madonna mit Kind und Heilige Anna, Öl auf Holz
Vierge à l'Enfant avec sainte Anne, huile sur bois
Madonna met Kind en Sint Anna, olieverf op paneel
1508-1513
168 x 130 cm / 66.1 x 51.1 in.
Musée du Louvre, Paris

▶ **Leonardo da Vinci**
(Vinci, Firenze 1452 - Amboise 1519)
Lady with an Ermine, oil on wood
Dame mit dem Hermelin, Öl auf Holz
La Dame à l'hermine, huile sur bois
Dame met de hermelijn, olieverf op paneel
1488-1490
55 x 40,5 cm / 21.6 x 15.9 in
Muzeum Czartoryski, Kraków

Leonardo da Vinci
(Vinci, Firenze 1452 - Amboise 1519)
Self-Portrait, red chalk on paper
Selbstbildnis, Rötel auf Papier
Autoportrait, sanguine sur papier
Zelfportret, Rood krijt op papier
c. 1512
33,3 x 21,3 cm / 13.1 x 8.3 in.
Biblioteca Reale, Torino

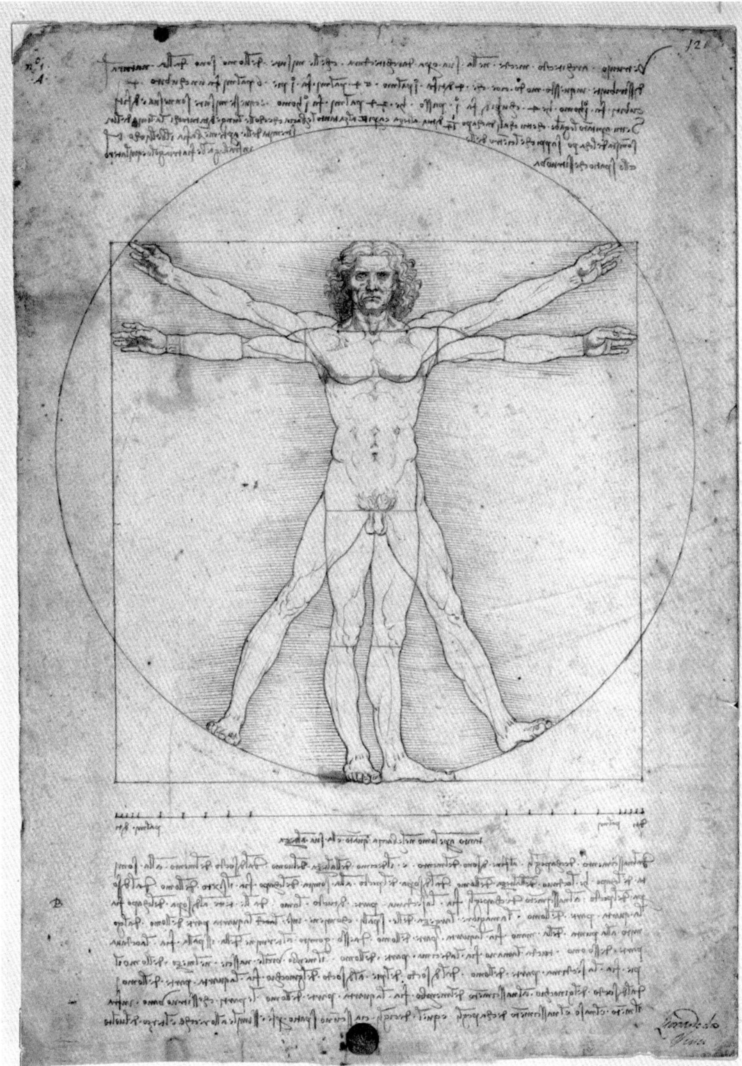

Leonardo da Vinci
(Vinci, Firenze 1452 - Amboise 1519)
Proportions of the Human Body according to Vitruvius, metal graver, pen, ink and watercolour on paper
Der Vetruvianischer Mensch, Metallspitze, Feder, Tinte und Aquarell auf Papier
L'Homme de Vitruve, pointe métallique, plume, encre et aquarelle sur papier
De verhoudingen van het menselijk lichaam volgens Vitruvius, metalen punt, pen, inkt en aquarel op papier
c. 1490
34,4 x 24,5 cm / 13.5 x 9.6 in
Gallerie dell'Accademia, Venezia

Leonardo da Vinci
(Vinci, Firenze 1452 - Amboise 1519)
Last Supper, tempera and oil on plaster
Das letzte Abendmahl, Tempera und Öl auf Putz
La Cène, détrempe et huile sur enduit
Het Laatse Avondmaal, tempera en olieverf op pleisterwerk
1494-1498
460 x 880 cm / 181.1 x 346.4 in.
Santa Maria delle Grazie, Milano

▶ **Leonardo da Vinci**
(Vinci, Firenze 1452 - Amboise 1519)
Mona Lisa, oil on wood
Die Mona Lisa, Öl auf Holz
La Joconde, huile sur bois
De Mona Lisa, olieverf op paneel
1503-1506
77 x 53 cm / 30.3 x 20.8 in.
Musée du Louvre, Paris

■ *"Present your figures in such a posture as to demonstrate what occupies the spirit of the figure; otherwise your art will merit no praise."*
■ *"Du wirst die Gestalten derart formen, dass sie hinreichend aufzeigen, was die Gestalt in sich birgt; andernfalls ist deine Kunst nicht lobenswert."*
■ *«Tu feras les personnages de façon à montrer ce qu'un personnage a dans l'esprit ; autrement, ton art ne sera pas digne de louange.»*
■ *"Je dient je figuren dusdanig af te beelden, dat er voldoende wordt getoond wat het figuur in zijn gedachten heeft; anders zal jouw kunst niet lovenswaardig zijn."*
Leonardo da Vinci

Luca Signorelli
(Cortona, Arezzo 1445 - 1523)
The Damned Cast into Hell, fresco
Die Verdammten in der Hölle, Fresko
Les Damnés, fresque
Verdoemden in de Hel, fresco
1499-1502
49 x 39 cm / 19.2 x 15.3 in.
Duomo, Orvieto

◀ **Domenico Ghirlandaio**
(Firenze 1449 - 1494)
Old Man with his Grandchild, tempera on wood
Alter Mann mit seinem Enkel, Tempera auf Holz
Portrait d'un vieillard et d'un jeune garçon, détrempe sur bois
Oude man met kleinzoon, tempera op paneel
c. 1490
62 x 46 cm / 24.4 x 18.1 in.
Musée du Louvre, Paris

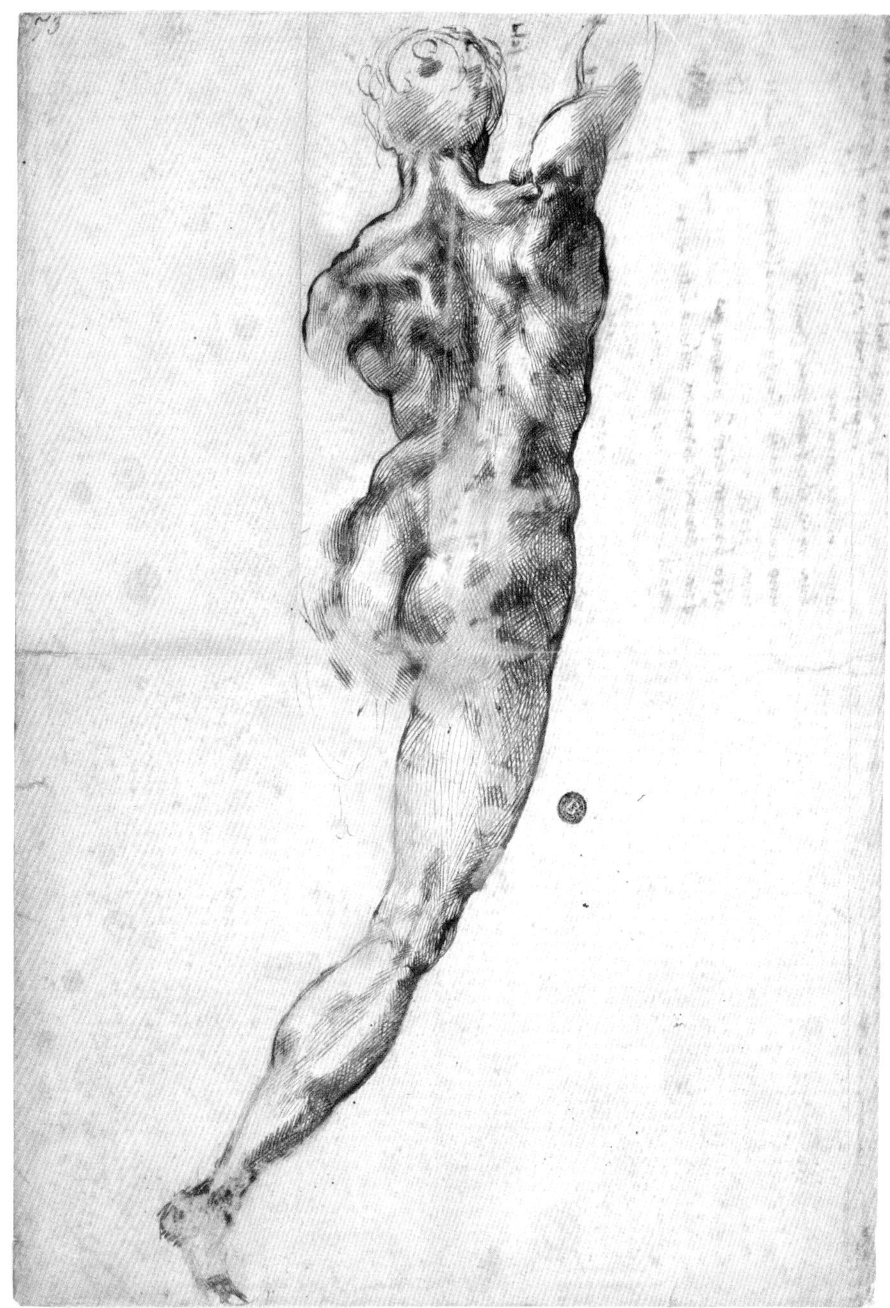

◀ **Michelangelo Buonarroti**
(Caprese, Arezzo 1475 - Roma 1564)
Male Nude Seen from the Back, pen and traces of pencil on paper
Rückenakt, Feder und Bleistiftspuren auf Papier
Homme nu, vu de dos, plume et traces de crayon sur papier
Naakte man vanaf de achterkant, pen en potloodschetsen op papier
c. 1504-1505
40,8 x 28,4 cm / 16 x 11.1 in.
Casa Buonarroti, Firenze

Michelangelo Buonarroti
(Caprese, Arezzo 1475 - Roma 1564)
Holy Family (Tondo Doni), tempera on wood
Die Heilige Familie (Tondo Doni), Tempera auf Holz
La Sainte Famille (Tondo Doni), détrempe sur bois
Heilige Familie (Tondo Doni), tempera op paneel
1504-1506
ø 120 cm / 47.2 in.
Galleria degli Uffizi, Firenze

Michelangelo Buonarroti
(Caprese, Arezzo 1475 - Roma 1564)
Ceiling of the *Sistine Chapel*, fresco
Gewölbe der *Sixtinischen Kapelle*, Fresko
Voûte de la *Chapelle Sixtine*, fresque
Gewelf van de *Sixtijnse Kapel*, fresco
1508-1512
Palazzi Vaticani, Città del Vaticano

▶ **Michelangelo Buonarroti**
(Caprese, Arezzo 1475 - Roma 1564)
The Delphic Sybil, fresco
Sibylle von Delphi, Fresko
Sybille de Delphes, fresque
De Delphische Sibille, fresco
1508-1512
Cappella Sistina, Palazzi Vaticani, Città del Vaticano

Michelangelo Buonarroti
(Caprese, Arezzo 1475 - Roma 1564)
The Creation of Adam, fresco
Die Erschaffung Adams, Fresko
Création d'Adam, fresque
De schepping van Adam, fresco
1508-1512
Cappella Sistina, Palazzi Vaticani, Città del Vaticano

▶ **Michelangelo Buonarroti**
(Caprese, Arezzo 1475 - Roma 1564)
The Last Judgment, fresco
Das Jüngste Gericht, Fresko
Le Jugement dernier, fresque
Het Laatste Oordeel, fresco
1534-1541
Cappella Sistina, Palazzi Vaticani, Città del Vaticano

"Painting is work of the mind and not of the hands."
"Man malt mit den Gehirn und nicht mit den Händen."
«On peint avec le cerveau, non avec les mains.»
"Men schildert met zijn hersens en niet met zijn handen."
Michelangelo Buonarroti

IONAS

Raffaello
(Urbino 1483 - Roma 1520)
Madonna del Belvedere, oil on wood
Madonna im Grünen, Öl auf Holz
La Madone du Belvédère, huile sur bois
Madonna van de Weide, olieverf op paneel
1505-1506
113 x 88,5 cm / 44.4 x 34.8 in.
Kunsthistorisches Museum, Wien

▶ **Raffaello**
(Urbino 1483 - Roma 1520)
Marriage of the Virgin, oil on wood
Die Hochzeit der Jungfrau, Öl auf Holz
Le Mariage de la Vierge, huile sur bois
Huwelijk van de Maagd, olieverf op paneel
1504
170 x 117 cm / 66.9 x 46 in.
Pinacoteca di Brera, Milano

RAPHAEL.VRBINAS
M. DIIII

Raffaello
(Urbino 1483 - Roma 1520)
The School of Athens, fresco
Die Schule von Athen, Fresko
L'École d'Athènes, fresque
School van Athene, fresco
1508-1511
Stanza della Segnatura, Palazzi Vaticani, Città del Vaticano

◀ **Raffaello**
(Urbino 1483 - Roma 1520)
Canigiani Holy Family, oil on wood
Heilige Familie Canigiani, Öl auf Holz
La Sainte Famille Canigiani, huile sur bois
Heilige Familie van het huis Canigiani, olieverf op paneel
c. 1507
131 x 107 cm / 51.5 x 42.1 in.
Alte Pinakothek, München

"Here lies Raffaello: while he lived Nature feared defeat; now that he is dead, she is afraid to die."
"Hier ruht Raffael: zu Lebzeiten fürchtete die Natur, von ihm besiegt zu werden, jetzt, wo er tot ist, fürchtet sie zu sterben."
«Ici gît Raphäel : par lui, de son vivant, la nature craignit d'être vaincue ; aujourd'hui il est mort et elle craint de mourir.»
"Hier ligt Rafaël; de grote Moeder Natuur vreesde bij zijn leven door hem te zullen worden overtroffen, bij zijn dood vreest ze met hem te zullen sterven."
Pietro Bembo

Raffaello
(Urbino 1483 - Roma 1520)
Madonna Sistina, oil on canvas
Sixtinische Madonna, Öl auf Leinwand
La Madone Sixtine, huile sur toile
Sixtijnse Madonna, olieverf op doek
1512-1513
269,5 x 201 cm / 106.1 x 79.1 in.
Gemäldegalerie Alte Meister, Staatliche Kunstsammlungen, Dresden

Raffaello
(Urbino 1483 - Roma 1520)
Madonna della seggiola, oil on wood
Madonna auf dem Stuhle, Öl auf Holz
La Vierge à la chaise, huile sur bois
Madonna met de stoel, olieverf op paneel
c. 1513-1514
ø 71 cm / 27.9 in.
Galleria Palatina, Firenze

Pontormo
(Pontorme, Empoli 1494 - Firenze 1556)
Deposition, oil on wood
Kreuzabnahme, Öl auf Holz
Déposition de Croix, huile sur bois
Kruisafneming, olieverf op paneel
1525
313 x 192 cm / 123.2 x 75.6 in.
Santa Felicita, Firenze

Agnolo Bronzino
(Firenze 1503 - 1572)
Portrait of Lucrezia Pucci Panciatichi, oil on wood
Porträt der Lucrezia Pucci Panciatichi, Öl auf Holz
Portrait de Lucrezia Pucci Panciatichi, huile sur bois
Portret van Lucretia Pucci Panciatichi, olieverf op paneel
c. 1540
101 x 82,8 cm / 39.7 x 32.5 in.
Galleria degli Uffizi, Firenze

Agnolo Bronzino
(Firenze 1503 - 1572)
Portrait of Bia de' Medici, oil on wood
Porträt der Bia de' Medici, Öl auf Holz
Portrait de Bia de Médicis, huile sur bois
Portret van Bia de' Medici, olieverf op paneel
c.1542
64 x 48 cm / 25.1 x 18.8 in.
Galleria degli Uffizi, Firenze

6

Painting in Northern Italy

As the artistic theories of the Renaissance began to be known, the painting of Northern Italy developed new models of expression through the works of such masters as Antonello da Messina, Giovanni e Gentile Bellini, Mantegna, Carpaccio and Tiziano. The region of Veneto, together with Lombardia and Emilia, represented the vigorous centre and, by means of tonal painting, focused particular attention on light, which mingled at times with classicism and at times with the Flemish tradition.

Die Malerei in Norditalien

Mit der Anwendung und Verbreitung der künstlerischen Studien der Renaissance entwickelt die Malerei in Norditalien neue Ausdrucksmodelle, wobei dies Meistern wie Antonello di Messina, Giovanni und Gentile Bellini, Mantegna, Carpaccio und Tizian zu verdanken ist. Mit der Ton-in-Ton Malerei bringt Venetien, das mit der Lombardei und der Emilia ein leuchtendes Zentrum darstellt, dem Licht ein besonderes Interesse entgegen, das sich bald mit den neuen Einflüssen des Klassizismus, bald mit jenen der flämischen Malerei verbindet.

La peinture dans l'Italie du Nord

Avec l'apport et la diffusion des recherches artistiques de la Renaissance, la peinture de l'Italie du Nord développe de nouveaux modèles d'expression, grâce à des maîtres comme Antonello de Messine, Giovanni et Gentile Bellini, Mantegna, Carpaccio, Giorgione et Titien. À côté de la Lombardie et de l'Émilie, la Vénétie constitue le centre le plus brillant de cet art renouvelé : sa peinture accorde une attention toute particulière à la lumière, qui se mêle tantôt aux suggestions du classicisme, tantôt à celles de la peinture flamande.

Schilderkunst in Noord-Italië

Met de tot stand brenging en de verspreiding van de renaissancistische artistieke studies, ontwikkelde de schilderkunst van Noord-Italië nieuwe expressieve modellen, met dank aan meesters als Antonello da Messina, Giovanni en Gentile Bellini, Mantegna, Carpaccio en Titiaan. Veneto, grenzend aan Lombardije en Emilia, omvat het meest lichtende centrum en vestigt met de tonale schilderkunst bijzondere aandacht op het licht, dat zich soms versmelt met de nieuwe invloeden van het Classicisme en soms met de inlvoeden van de Vlaamse schilderkunst.

Pisanello
(Pisa *c.* 1380 - ante 1455)
Departure of St. George, detail of St. George and the Princess, fresco
Abfahrt des Hl. Georg, Detail mit Hl. Georg und die Prinzessin, Fresko
Départ de saint Georges, détail avec saint Georges et la princesse, fresque
Het vertrek van Sint Joris, detail van Sint Joris met de prinses, fresco
1433-1438
223 x 620 cm / 87.7 x 244 in.
Sant'Anastasia, Verona

Cosmè Tura
(Ferrara c. 1430 - 1495)
Madonna of the Zodiac, tempera on wood
Madonna mit Kind, Tempera auf Holz
Vierge à l'Enfant, détrempe sur bois
Madonna van de Dierenriem, tempera op paneel
1459-1463
61 x 41 cm / 24 x 16.1 in.
Gallerie dell'Accademia, Venezia

Carlo Crivelli
(Venezia 1430/1435 - Ascoli Piceno 1494/1500)
Madonna of the Passion, tempera on wood
Madonna della Passione, Tempera auf Holz
Vierge de la Passion, détrempe sur bois
Madonna van de Passie, tempera op paneel
c. 1460
71 x 48 cm / 27.9 x 18.8 in.
Museo di Castelvecchio, Verona

Andrea Mantegna
(Isola di Carturo, Padova 1431 - Mantova 1506)
Saint George, tempera on wood
Heiliger Georg, Tempera auf Holz
Saint Georges, détrempe sur bois
Sint Joris, tempera op paneel
c. 1460
66 x 32 cm / 25.9 x 12.5 in.
Gallerie dell'Accademia, Venezia

Andrea Mantegna
(Isola di Carturo, Padova 1431 - Mantova 1506)
San Zeno Altarpiece: predella with the *Crucifixion*, tempera on wood
Altarbild San Zeno: Altarsockel mit der *Kreuzugung*, Tempera auf Holz
Retable de San Zeno: détail de la prédelle avec *La Crucifixion*, détrempe sur bois
Altaarstuk van San Zeno: predella met de *Kruisiging*, tempera op paneel
1456-1459
76 x 96 cm / 29.9 x 37.7 in.
Musée du Louvre, Paris

▶ **Andrea Mantegna**
(Isola di Carturo, Padova 1431 - Mantova 1506)
Court Scene, detail of Ludovico III and his Family, fresco
Hofszene, Detail mit Lodovico III. und der Familie, Fresko
Scène de cour, détail avec *Louis III et sa famille*, fresque
Hofscène: detail met Ludovico III Gonzaga en de familie, fresco
1465-1474
Camera degli Sposi, Palazzo Ducale, Mantova

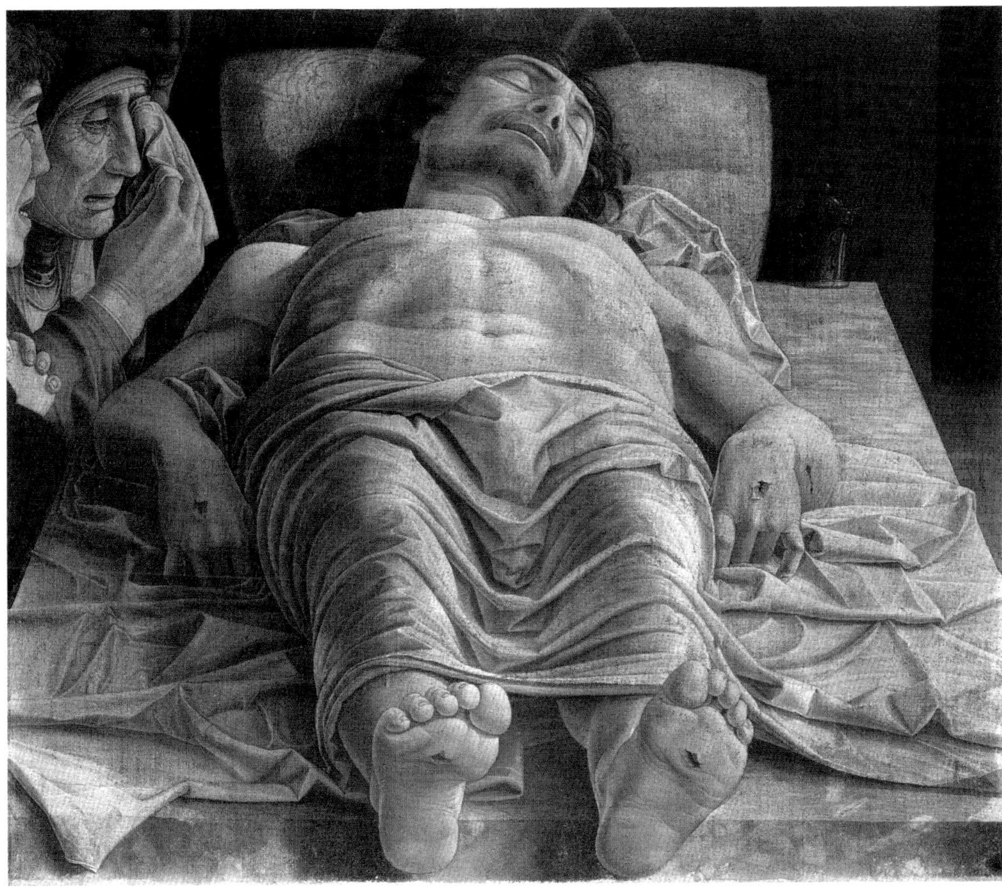

Andrea Mantegna
(Isola di Carturo, Padova 1431 - Mantova 1506)
Dead Christ, tempera on canvas
Der tote Christus, Tempera auf Leinwand
Le Christ mort, détrempe sur toile
Dode Christus, tempera op doek
c. 1480-1490
66 x 81 cm / 25.9 x 31.8 in.
Pinacoteca di Brera, Milano

◀ **Andrea Mantegna**
(Isola di Carturo, Padova 1431 - Mantova 1506)
Central Oculus of the Ceiling, fresco
Zentrales Schein-Opaion an der Decke, Fresko
Oculus en trompe-l'œil du plafond, fresque
Oculus in het midden van het plafond, fresco
1465-1474
ø 270 cm / 106.2 in.
Camera degli Sposi, Palazzo Ducale, Mantova

Antonello da Messina
(Messina c. 1430 - 1479)
The Virgin Annunciate, tempera and oil on wood
Maria der Verkündigung, Tempera und Öl auf Holz
Vierge de l'Annonciation, détrempe et huile sur bois
Maria-boodschap, tempera en olieverf op paneel
c. 1476
45 x 34,5 cm / 17.7 x 13.5 in.
Galleria Regionale della Sicilia

▶ **Antonello da Messina**
(Messina c. 1430 - 1479)
Saint Jerome in his Study, oil on wood
Heiliger Hieronymus im Gehäuse, Öl auf Holz
Saint Jérôme dans son cabinet de travail, huile sur bois
Sint Hiëronymus in zijn studeerkamer, olieverf op paneel
c. 1475
45,7 x 36,2 cm / 17.9 x 14.2 in.
National Gallery, London

Giovanni Bellini
(Venezia c. 1432 - 1516)
Madonna and Child (Sacra Conversazione Giovanelli), oil on wood
Sacra Conversazione Giovanelli, Öl auf Holz
Sainte Conversation Giovanelli, huile sur bois
Sacra Conversazione Giovanelli (Het Heilige Gesprek), olieverf op paneel
1500-1504
54 x 76 cm / 21.2 x 29.9 in.
Gallerie dell'Accademia, Venezia

Giovanni Bellini
(Venezia c. 1432 - 1516)
Pietà
Oil on wood
Öl auf Holz
Huile sur bois
Olieverf op paneel
c. 1505
65 x 90 cm / 25.5 x 35.4 in.
Gallerie dell'Accademia, Venezia

Gentile Bellini
(Venezia 1429 - 1507)
Procession in St. Mark's Square, tempera on canvas
Prozession auf dem Markusplatz, Tempera auf Leinwand
Procession sur la place Saint-Marc, détrempe sur toile
Processie op de Piazzo San Marco, tempera op doek
c. 1496
367,5 x 746 cm / 144.6 x 293.7 in.
Gallerie dell'Accademia, Venezia

Vittore Carpaccio
(Venezia c. 1460 - 1526)
Stories of St. Ursula: Dream of St. Ursula, tempera on canvas
Geschichten der Heiligen Ursula: Traum der Heiligen Ursula, Tempera auf Leinwand
Le Songe de sainte Ursule, détrempe sur toile
Legende van de Heilige Ursula: Droom van Ursula, tempera op doek
1495
274 x 267 cm / 107.8 x 105.1 in.
Gallerie dell'Accademia, Venezia

▶ **Vittore Carpaccio**
(Venezia c. 1460 - 1526)
Two Venetian Ladies, tempera and oil on wood
Venezianische Damen, Tempera und Öl auf Holz
Les Deux Dames vénitiennes, détrempe et huile sur bois
Venetiaanse dames, tempera en olieverf op paneel
c. 1495
94 x 64 cm / 37 x 25.1 in.
Museo Correr, Venezia

Giorgione
(Castelfranco Veneto, Treviso 1477/1478 - Venezia 1510)
Sleeping Venus, oil on canvas
Die schlafende Venus, Öl auf Leinwand
Vénus endormie, huile sur toile
Slapende Venus, olieverf op doek
1508-1510
108,5 x 175 cm / 42.7 x 68.8 in.
Gemäldegalerie Alte Meister, Staatliche Kunstsammlungen, Dresden

▶ **Giorgione**
(Castelfranco Veneto, Treviso 1477/1478 - Venezia 1510)
The Tempest, oil on canvas
Der Sturm, Öl auf Leinwand
La Tempête, huile sur toile
Het onweer, olieverf op doek
c. 1505
82 x 73 cm / 32.2 x 28.7 in.
Gallerie dell'Accademia, Venezia

Tiziano Vecellio
(Pieve di Cadore, Belluno c. 1490 - Venezia 1576)
Sacred and Profane Love, oil on wood
Die himmlische und die irdische Liebe, Öl auf Leinwand
L'Amour sacré et l'Amour profane, huile sur toile
De Heilige en de Profane liefde, olieverf op doek
c. 1514
118 x 279 cm / 46.4 x 109.8 in.
Galleria Borghese, Roma

"No other great artist took so much from others while making so few concessions [as Tiziano]; no other great artist was so flexible while always remaining completely himself."

"Kein anderer großer Künstler [wie Tiziano] nahm soviel mit sowenig Zugeständnissen auf; kein anderer großer Künstler war so anpassungsfähig, und dennoch immer ganz er selbst."

«Aucun autre grand artiste [comme Titien] ne s'appropria tant de choses en faisant si peu de concessions ; aucun autre artiste ne fut aussi souple tout en restant complètement lui-même.»

"Geen andere grote kunstenaar [als Titiaan] nam zoveel, met zo weinig concessies; geen andere grote kunstenaar was zo enorm flexibel en bleef toch helemaal zichzelf."

Erwin Panofsky

Tiziano Vecellio
(Pieve di Cadore, Belluno c. 1490 - Venezia 1576
The Venus of Urbino, oil on canvas
Venus von Urbino, Öl auf Leinwand
La Vénus d'Urbino, huile sur toile
Venus van Urbino, olieverf op doek
1538
119 x 165 cm / 46.8 x64.9 in.
Galleria degli Uffizi, Firenze

▶ **Tiziano Vecellio**
(Pieve di Cadore, Belluno c. 1490 - Venezia 1576)
Flora
Oil on canvas
Öl auf Leinwand
Huile sur toile
Olieverf op doek
1515-1520
79,7 x 63,5 cm / 31.3 x 24.9 in.
Galleria degli Uffizi, Firenze

Tintoretto
(Venezia 1518 - 1594)
Susanna in the Bath, oil on canvas
Susanna im Bad, Öl auf Leinwand
Suzanne au bain, huile sur toile
Susanna in bad, olieverf op doek
c. 1555-1556
146 x 193,6 cm / 57.4 x 76.2 in.
Kunsthistorisches Museum, Wien

▶ **Paris Bordone**
(Treviso 1500 - Venezia 1571)
The Venetian Lovers, oil on canvas
Venezianisches Liebespaar, Öl auf Leinwand
Couple vénitien, huile sur toile
De Venetiaanse geliefden, olieverf op doek
1525-1530
81 x 86 cm / 31.8 x 33.8 in.
Pinacoteca di Brera, Milano

Paolo Veronese
(Verona 1528 - Venezia 1588)
The Marriage at Cana, oil on canvas
Die Hochzeit zu Kana, Öl auf Leinwand
Les Noces de Cana, huile sur toile
Bruiloft te Kana, olieverf op doek
1563
677 x 994 cm / 266.5 x 391.3 in.
Musée du Louvre, Paris

► **Paolo Veronese**
(Verona 1528 - Venezia 1588)
Giustina Giustinian Barbaro and her Nurse, fresco
Giustina Giustinian Barbaro und die Amme, Fresko
Giustina Giustinian Barbaro et sa nourrice, fresque
Giustina Giustinian Barbaro met de min, fresco
1560 -1561
Villa Barbaro, Maser

Parmigianino
(Parma 1503 - Cremona 1540)
Cupid Carving his Bow, oil on wood
Amor beim Schnitzen seines Bogens, Öl auf Holz
Amour taillant son arc, huile sur bois
Amor snijdt zijn boog, olieverf op paneel
1533-1534
135 x 65,3 cm / 53.1 x 25.7 in.
Kunsthistorisches Museum, Wien

► **Correggio**
(Correggio, Reggio Emilia 1489 - 1534)
Assumption of the Virgin, central part, fresco
Aufnahme der Jungfrau, zentraler Teil, Fresko
L'Assomption de la Vierge, détail avec la partie centrale, fresque
Maria-Tenhemelopneming, midden gedeelte, fresco
1526-1530
1093 x 1195 cm / 430.3 x 470.4 in.
Cathedral / Kathedrale / Cathédrale / Kathedraal, Parma

Lorenzo Lotto
(Venezia c. 1480 - Loreto 1556)
Portrait of a Lady as Lucretia, oil on canvas
Porträt einer Venezianerin als Lucrezia, Öl auf Leinwand
Portrait de dame en Lucrèce, huile sur toile
Portret van dame gekleed als Lucrezia, olieverf op doek
1530-1532
96,5 x 110,6 cm / 37.9 x 43.5 in.
National Gallery, London

▶ **Giulio Romano**
(Roma c. 1499 - Mantova 1546)
Olympus, fresco
Olympus, Fresko
L'Olympe, fresque
Olympus, fresco
1526-1535
Palazzo Te, Mantova

Painting in Europe

Such excellent painters as Fouquet, Van Eyck, Cranach, Dürer, Grünewald, Holbein and El Greco in France, Germany, Flanders and Spain represented the European Renaissance. With their masterpieces, including portraits and works with religious and mythological subjects, painting proposed modern elements based on the most recent Renaissance models, creating a modern concept of space and representation of reality.

Die Malerei in Europa

Die europäische Malerei kennt in Frankreich, Deutschland, Flandern und Spanien Maler ersten Ranges, wie Fouquet, Van Eyck, Cranach, Dürer, Grünewald, Holbein und El Greco. Mit ihren Meisterwerken, darunter Portraits und Werke religiösen und mythologischen Charakters, bietet die Malerei neue Stilrichtungen an, die sich an den neuesten Renaissancemodellen anlehnen, in denen sich ein modernes Konzept der Räumlichkeit und der Darstellung der Wirklichkeit abzeichnet.

7

La peinture en Europe

Partie d'Italie, la Renaissance voit naître en France et en Allemagne, en Flandre et en Espagne, des peintres de tout premier ordre avec des artistes comme Fouquet, Van Eyck, Cranach, Dürer, Grünewald, Holbein et le Gréco. Avec leurs chefs-d'œuvre, dont de nombreux portraits et des tableaux à sujets mythologiques ou sacrés, la peinture propose de nouvelles approches stylistiques, alignées sur les modèles Renaissance les plus avancés, où s'esquisse une conception moderne de l'espace et de la représentation du réel.

Schilderkunst in Europa

De Europese Renaissance kent in Frankrijk, Duitsland, Vlaanderen en Spanje eersteklas kunstenaars als Fouquet, Van Eyck, Cranach, Dürer, Grünewald, Holbein en El Greco. Met hun meesterwerken, waaronder portretten en werken met religieuze en mythologische karakters, boden zij de schilderkunst nieuwe gemoderniseerde stijlen, die zich baseerden op de nieuwste renaissancistische modellen, waarin een modern concept van ruimte en weergave van de werkelijkheid werd geschetst.

Jan van Eyck
(Maastricht c. 1390 - Brugge 1441)
Ghent Altarpiece, oil on wood
Polyptychon von Gent, Öl auf Holz
Polyptique de l'Agneau mystique, huile sur bois
Veelluik 'Het Lam Gods', olieverf op paneel
1432
350 x 223 cm / 137.7 x 87.7 in.
Saint Bavon, Gent

◀ **Jan van Eyck**
(Maastricht c. 1390 - Brugge 1441)
The Arnolfini Portrait, oil on wood
Die Arnolfini-Hochzeit, Öl auf Holz
Les Époux Arnolfini, huile sur bois
Portret van het echtpaar Arnolfini, olieverf op paneel
1434
82,2 x 60 cm / 32.3 x 23.6 in.
National Gallery, London

Rogier van der Weyden
(Tournai c. 1400 - Bruxelles 1464)
Deposition, oil on wood
Kreuzabnahme, Öl auf Holz
Descente de Croix, huile sur bois
Kruisafneming, olieverf op paneel
1435
220 x 262 cm / 86.6 x 103.1 in.
Museo del Prado, Madrid

▶ **Petrus Christus**
(Baerle c. 1420 - Brugge 1472/1473)
Portrait of a Young Girl, oil on wood
Porträt eines Mädchens, Öl auf Holz
Portrait de jeune fille, huile sur bois
Portret van een jonge edelvrouw, olieverf op paneel
c. 1470
29 x 23 cm / 11.4 x 9 in.
Gemäldegalerie, Staatliche Museen, Berlin

Hugo van der Goes
(Gent c. 1435/1440 - Rode Klooster, Bruxelles 1482)
Portinari Triptych: central panel with the *Adoration of the Shepherds*, oil on wood
Portinari-Triptychon: Mitteltafel mit der *Anbetung der Hirten*, Öl auf Holz
Tryptique Portinari : panneau central avec l'*Adoration des bergers*, huile sur bois
Portinari-drieluik: middenpaneel met de *Aanbidding der Herders*, olieverf op paneel
c. 1476
249 x 300 cm / 98.3 x 118.1 in.
Galleria degli Uffizi, Firenze

Hieronymus Bosch
(s'Hertogenbosch c. 1450 - 1516)
Seven Deadly Sins, oil on wood
Die Sieben Todsünden, Öl auf Holz
Les Sept Péchés capitaux, huile sur bois
De zeven hoofdzonden, olieverf op paneel
1475-1480
120 x 150 cm / 47.2 x 59 in.
Museo del Prado, Madrid

▶ **Hieronymus Bosch**
(s'Hertogenbosch c. 1450 - 1516)
Garden of Earthly Delights Triptych, oil on wood
Triptychon, der Garten der Lüste, Öl auf Holz
Le Jardin des Délices, huile sur bois
Drieluik van de Tuin der Lusten, olieverf op paneel
1503-1504
220 x 389 cm / 86.6 x 153.1 in.
Museo del Prado, Madrid

"The others attempt to depict men as they appear on the outside; this one dares to depict what they are inside."
"Die Anderen versuchen die Menschen so zu malen, wie sie von außen erscheinen, und dieser hat die Kühnheit, sie zu malen, wie sie drinnen sind."
« Les autres cherchent à peindre les hommes comme ils apparaissent vus de l'extérieur ; mais lui a la hardiesse de les peindre comme ils sont à l'intérieur. »
"Anderen trachten de mens te schilderen zoals hij aan de buitenkant is; en hij [Hieronymus Bosch] heeft de moed de mens te schilderen zoals hij van binnen is."
Juan de Siguenza

Hieronymus Bosch
(s'Hertogenbosch c. 1450 - 1516)
The Road to Calvary, oil on wood
Die Kreuztragung Christi, Öl auf Holz
La Montée au Calvaire, huile sur bois
De Kruisdraging, olieverf op paneel
1510-1516
74 x 81 cm / 29.1 x 31.8 in.
Museum voor Schone Kunsten, Gent

▶ **Mabuse**
(Maubeuge c. 1478 - Middelburg 1532)
Danae, oil on wood
Danae, Öl auf Holz
Danaé, huile sur bois
Danaë, olieverf op paneel
1527
95 x 114 cm / 37.4 x 44.8 in.
Alte Pinakothek, München

IOANNES MALBODIVS PINGEBAT 1527

Pieter Bruegel de Oude
(Breda 1528/1530 - Bruxelles 1569)
The Tower of Babel, oil on wood
Der Turmbau zu Babel, Öl auf Holz
La Tour de Babel, huile sur bois
De toren van Babel, olieverf op paneel
1563
114 x 155 cm / 44.8 x 61
Kunsthistorisches Museum, Wien

Albrecht Dürer
(Nürnberg 1471 - 1528)
Adam, oil on wood
Adam, Öl auf Holz
Adam, huile sur bois
Adam, olieverf op paneel
1507
209 x 81 cm / 82.2 x 31.8 in.
Museo del Prado, Madrid

Albrecht Dürer
(Nürnberg 1471 - 1528)
Eve, oil on wood
Eva, Öl auf Holz
Ève, huile sur bois
Eva, olieverf op paneel
1507
209 x 81 cm / 82.2 x 31.8 in.
Museo del Prado, Madrid

Matthias Grünewald
(Würzburg c. 1480 - Halle 1528)
Isenheim Altarpiece: The Crucifixion, oil on wood
Isenheimer Altar: Die Kreuzigung, Öl auf Holz
Le Retable d'Issenheim : la Crucifixion, huile sur bois
Isenheimer Altaar: De Kruisiging, olieverf op paneel
1512-1515
345 x 458 cm / 135.8 x 180.3 in.
Musée d'Unterlinden, Colmar

Lucas Cranach
(Kronach 1472 - Weimar 1553)
Three Saxon Princesses, Sibylla, Emilia and Sidonia, oil on wood
Porträt der Prinzessinen Sibylle, Emilia und Sidonia von Sachsen, Öl auf Holz
Les Princesses Sibylla, Emilia et Sidonia de Saxe, huile sur bois
Portret van de prinsessen Sybilla, Emilia en Sidonia van Saksen, olieverf op paneel
c. 1535
62 x 89 cm / 24.4 x 35 in.
Kunsthistorisches Museum, Wien

◀ **Albrecht Altdorfer**
(Regensburg c. 1480 - 1538)
The Battle of Alexander at Issus, oil on wood
Die Alexanderschlacht bei Issus, Öl auf Holz
La Bataille d'Issos, huile sur bois
De slag bij Issus, olieverf op paneel
1528-1529
158 x 120 cm / 62.2 x 47.2 in.
Alte Pinakothek, München

Hans Holbein der Jüngere
(Augsburg 1497/1498 - London 1543)
The Ambassadors, oil on wood
Die Botschafter, Öl auf Holz
Les Ambassadeurs, huile sur bois
De Ambassadeurs, olieverf op paneel
1533
207 x 209,5 cm / 81.4 x 82.4 in.
National Gallery, London

▶ **Hans Holbein der Jüngere**
(Augsburg 1497/1498 - London 1543)
Portrait of Henry VIII, oil on wood
Porträt von Heinrich VIII, Öl auf Holz
Henri VIII, huile sur bois
Portret van Hendrik VIII, olieverf op paneel
1540
88,5 x 74,5 cm / 34.8 x 29.3 in.
Galleria Nazionale di Arte Antica di Palazzo Barberini, Roma

· ANNO · ÆTATIS · · SVÆ · XLIX ·

Giuseppe Arcimboldo
(Milano 1527 - 1593)
Summer, oil on canvas
Der Sommer, Öl auf Leinwand
L'Été, huile sur toile
De Zomer, olieverf op doek
1563-1566
76 x 64 cm / 29.9 x 25.1 in.
Kunsthistorisches Museum, Wien

Jean Fouquet
(Tours c. 1425 - c. 1480)
Melun Diptych: right wing with the *Virgin and Child surrounded by Angels*, tempera on wood
Diptychon von Melun: Altarbild der *Madonna mit Kind und Cherubim*, Tempera auf Holz
Diptyque de Melun : volet avec la *Vierge à l'Enfant, et des chérubins*, détrempe sur bois
Diptiek van Melun: paneel met de *Madonna met het Kind en cherubijnen*, tempera op paneel
c. 1450
91 x 81 cm / 35.8 x 31.8 in.
Koninklijk Museum voor Schone Kunsten, Antwerpen

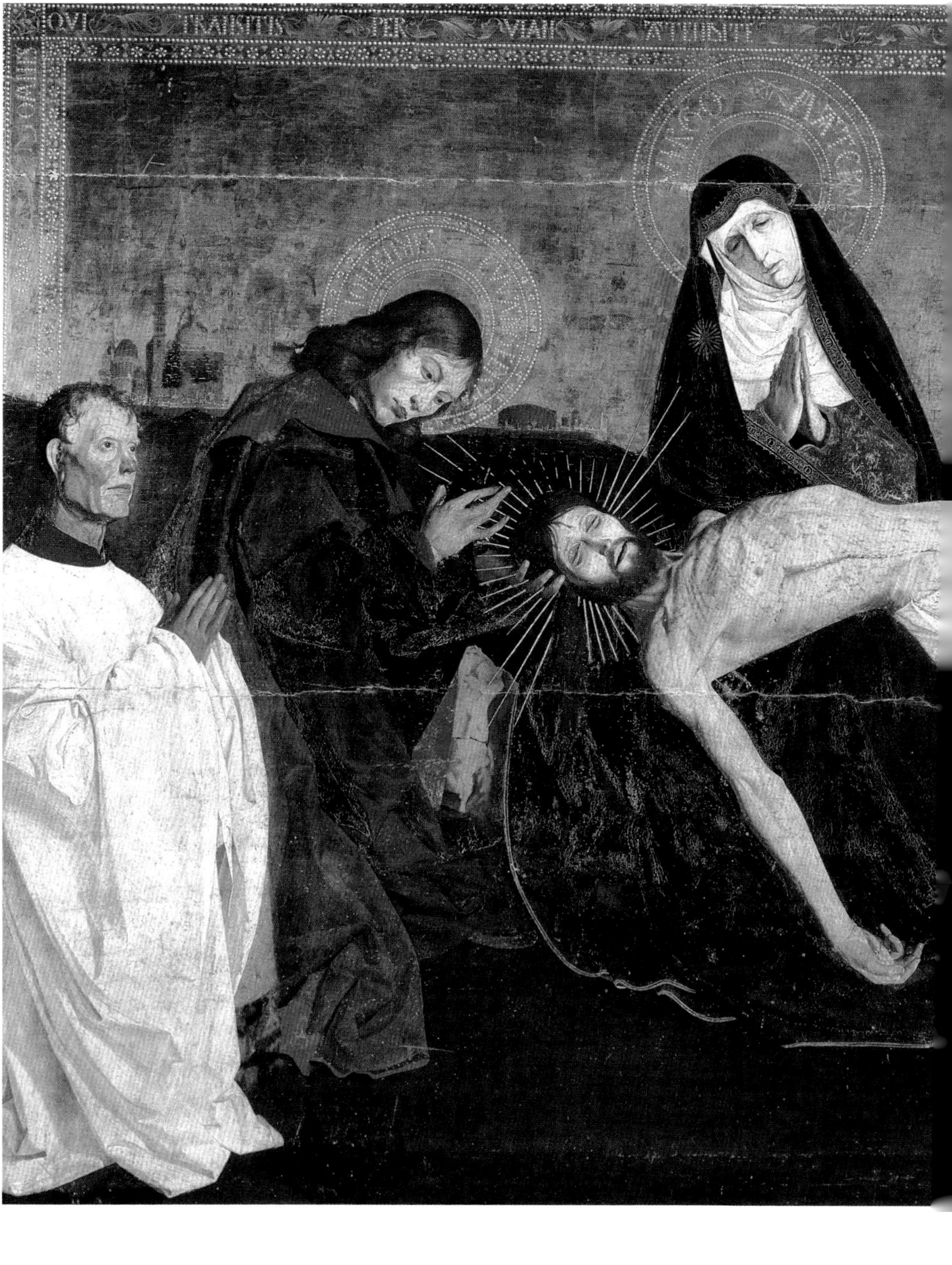

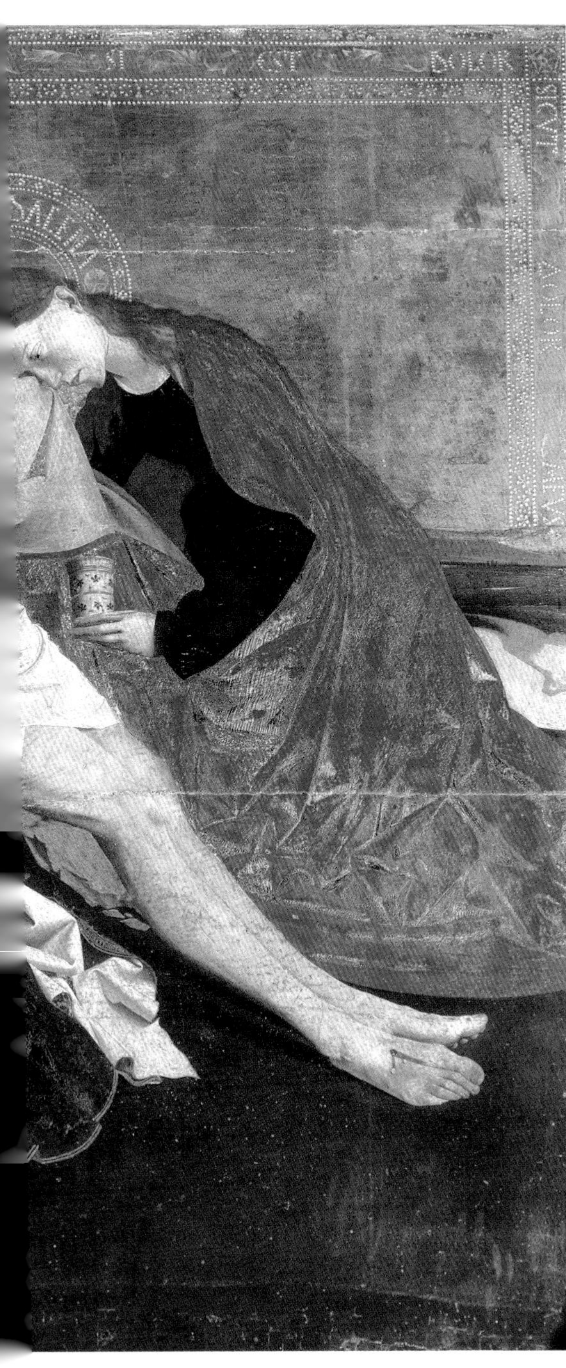

Enguerrand Quarton
(Laon 1410 - c. 1466)
The Avignon Pietà, tempera on wood
Die Pietà von Villeneuve-lès-Avignon, Tempera auf Holz
La Pietà de Villeneuve-lès-Avignon, détrempe sur bois
Pietà uit Villeneuve-lès-Avignon, tempera op paneel
c. 1455
163 x 218 cm / 64.1 x 85.8 in.
Musée du Louvre, Paris

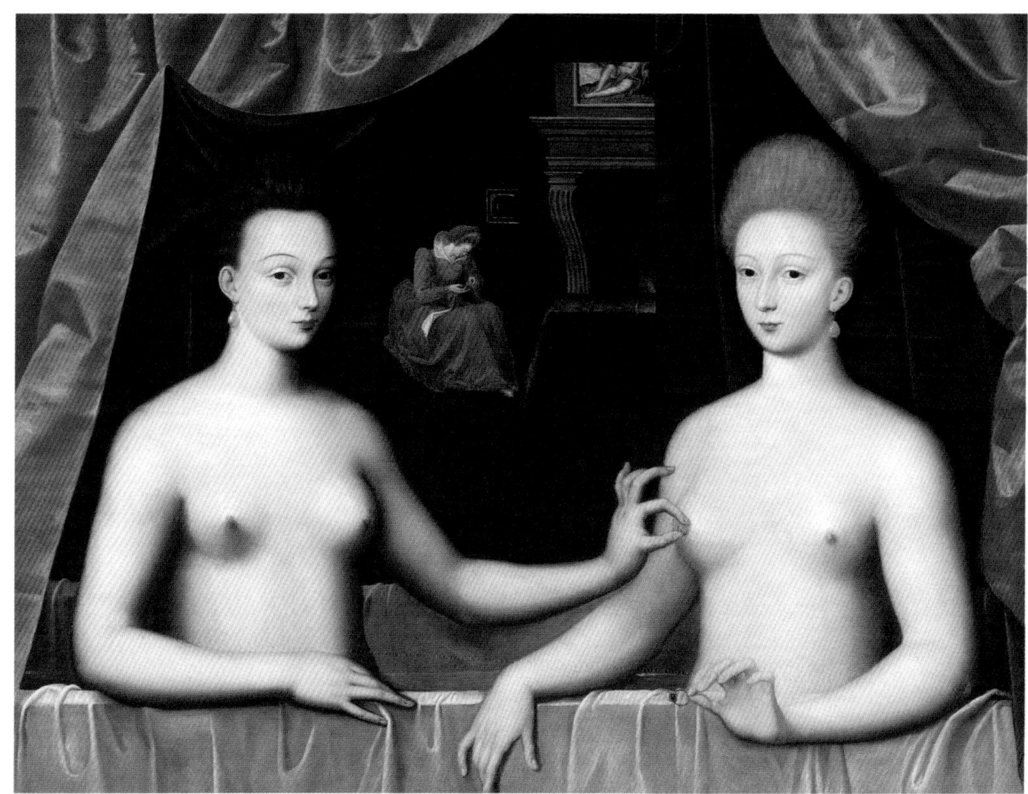

Portrait of Gabrielle d'Estrées and her Sister, the Duchess of Villars (presumed), oil on canvas
Bildnis der Gabrielle d'Estrées und ihre Schwester, die Herzogin von Villars, Öl auf Leinwand
Portrait présumé de Gabrielle d'Estrées et de sa sœur, la duchesse de Villars, huile sur toile
Vermeend portret van Gabrielle d'Estrées en haar zus, de hertogin van Villars, olieverf op doek
c. 1594
96 x 125 cm / 37.7 x 49.2 in.
Musée du Louvre, Paris

▶ **Jaime Huguet**
(Valls 1412 - Barcelona 1492)
Consecration of St. Augustine, tempera on wood
Weihe des Hl. Augustinus, Tempera auf Holz
Consécration de saint Augustin (Retable de Blanquer), détrempe sur bois
Consecratie van Sint Augustinus, tempera op paneel
1463-1485
272 x 200 cm / 107 x 78.7 in.
Museu Nacional d'Art de Catalunya, Barcelona

El Greco
(Candia 1541 - Toledo 1614)
Baptism of Christ, oil on canvas
Taufe Christi, Öl auf Leinwand
Le Baptême du Christ, huile sur toile
De Doop van Christus, olieverf op doek
c. 1597
111 x 47 cm / 43.7 x 18.5 in.
Galleria Nazionale d'Arte Antica di Palazzo Barberini, Roma

▶ **El Greco**
(Candia 1541 - Toledo 1614)
Christ clasping the Cross, oil on canvas
Christus trägt das Kreuz, Öl auf Leinwand
Le Christ portant sa croix, huile sur toile
Christus met het kruis, olieverf op doek
c. 1580
105 x 79 cm / 41.3 x 31.1 in.
Metropolitan Museum of Art, New York

Masterpieces of Renaissance Painting
Meisterwerke der Renaissance-Malerei
Chefs-d'œuvre de la peinture de la Renaissance
Meesterwerken van de schilderkunst van de Renaissance

Jan van Eyck
The Arnolfini Portrait
Die Arnolfini-Hochzeit
Portrait des époux Arnolfini
Portret van het echtpaar Arnolfini
1434
National Gallery, London

Piero della Francesca
Portraits of Federico da Montefeltro and Battista Sforza, dukes of Urbino
Diptychon des Federico da Montefeltro mi seiner Gattin Battista Sforza, Herzöge von Urbino
Portraits de Federico da Montefeltro et Battista, ducs d'Urbino
Portret van Federico da Montefeltro en Battista Sforza, hertogin van Urbino
c. 1465
Galleria degli Uffizi, Firenze

Sandro Botticelli
Birth of Venus
Geburt der Venus
La naissance de Vénus
Geboorte van Venus
1484-1485
Galleria degli Uffizi, Firenze

1400 1420 1440 1460 1480

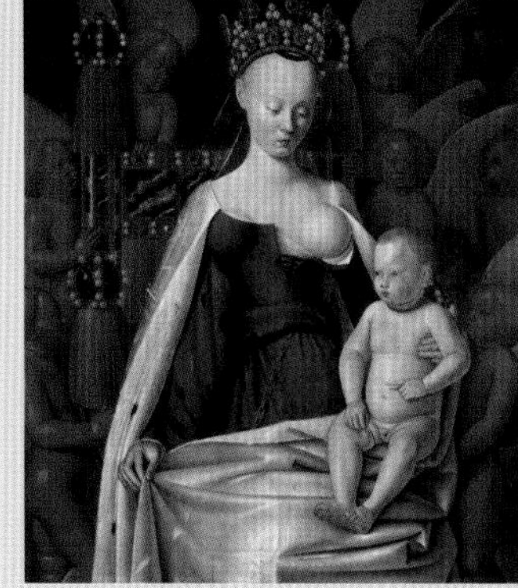

Jean Fouquet
Melun Diptych: right wing with the *Virgin and Child surrounded by Angels*
Diptychon von Melun: Altarbild der *Madonna mit Kind und Cherubim*
Diptyque de Melun: panneau avec la *Vierge à l'enfant entourée d'anges*
Diptiek van Melun: paneel met de *Madonna met het Kind en cherubijnen*
c. 1450
Koninklijk Museum voor Schone Kunsten, Antwerpen

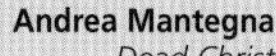

Andrea Mantegna
Dead Christ
Der tote Christus
Christ mort
Dode Christus
c. 1483
Pinacoteca di Brera, Milano

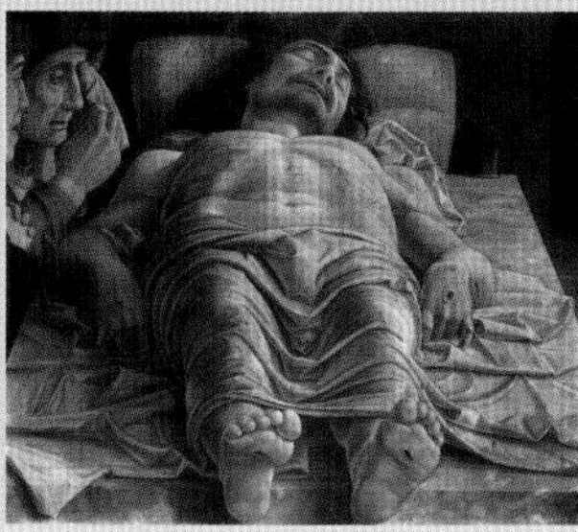

Leonardo da Vinci
Mona Lisa
Die Mona Lisa
La Joconde
De Mona Lisa
1503-1506
Musée du Louvre, Paris

Raffaello
Madonna della seggiola
Madonna auf dem Stuhle
Madone de la chaise
Madonna met de stoel
c. 1513-1514
Galleria Palatina, Firenze

1500 1520 1540 1560 1580

Michelangelo Buonarroti
Holy Family (Tondo Doni)
Die Heilige Familie (Tondo Doni)
Sainte famille à la tribune (Tondo Doni)
Heilige Familie (Tondo Doni)
1504-1506
Galleria degli Uffizi, Firenze

Albrecht Dürer
Adam
1507
Museo del Prado, Madrid

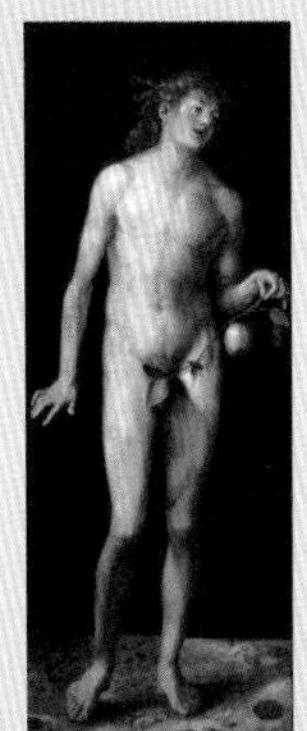

Tiziano Vecellio
The Venus of Urbino
Die Venus von Urbino
Vénus d'Urbin
Venus van Urbino
1538
Galleria degli Uffizi, Firenze

Chronology
Chronologie

1401	▮ Competition for the Baptistery doors in Firenze.	▮ Wettbewerb für die Pforte des Baptisteriums in Florenz.	▮ Concours pour la porte du Baptistère de Florence.	▮ Wedstrijd voor de deur van het Baptisterium van Florence.
1415	▮ Henry V of England defeated the French at the battle of Agincourt .	▮ Heinrich V von England besiegt die Franzosen in der Schlacht von Azincourt.	▮ Henri V d'Angleterre écrase les Français à la bataille d'Azincourt.	▮ Hendrik V van Engeland verslaat de Fransen bij de Slag bij Azincourt.
1418	▮ The Council of Costanza ended the great schism of the West. Brunelleschi won the competition for the dome of the cathedral in Firenze.	▮ Der Rat von Konstanz beendet die Spaltung des Westen. Brunelleschi gewinnt den Wettbewerb für die Kuppel der Santa Maria del Fiore in Florenz.	▮ Le concile de Constance met fin au schisme d'Occident. Brunelleschi remporte le concours pour la coupole de Santa Maria del Fiore, à Florence.	▮ Het Concilie van Konstanz maakt een einde aan het Westers Schisma. Brunelleschi wint de wedstrijd voor de koepel van de Santa Maria del Fiore in Florence.
1424-1427	▮ Masaccio and Masolino painted the frescos in the Brancacci chapel, in the Santa Maria del Carmine church in Firenze.	▮ Masaccio und Masolino malen die Fresken der Brancacci Kapelle in Santa Maria del Carmine in Florenz.	▮ Masaccio et Masolino exécutent les fresques de la chapelle Brancacci de Santa Maria del Carmine, à Florence.	▮ Masaccio en Masolino verwezenlijken fresco's voor de Brancacci Kapel in de Santa Maria del Carmine in Florence.
1431	▮ Martyrdom of Joan of Arc; coronation of Charles VII in Reims.	▮ Martyrium der Johanna von Orléans und des gekrönten Karl VII in Reims.	▮ Martyre de Jeanne d'Arc et couronnement de Charles VII à Reims.	▮ Marteling Jeanne d'Arc en kroning van Karel VII in Reims.
1434	▮ Jan van Eyck painted the *Arnolfini Portrait*. Donatello finished the *David* of bronze, now in the Bargello museum.	▮ Jan van Eyck malt Die *Arnolfini-Hochzeit*. Donatello gestaltet den *David* aus Bronze, heute im Bargello.	▮ Jan van Eyck peint *Arnolfini et sa femme* (ou *Les époux Arnolfini*). Donatello réalise le *David* en bronze qui se trouve aujourd'hui au musée du Bargello, à Florence.	▮ Jan van Eyck schildert *Het portret van Giovanni Arnolfini en zijn vrouw*. Donatello verwezenlijkt de bronzen *David*, vandaag de dag in Bargello.
1439	▮ The council to discuss unification of the Eastern and Western Churches was held in Firenze.	▮ In Florenz hält man ein Konzil und diskutiert über das Einigungsabkommen zwischen der lateinischen und der griechischen Kirche.	▮ À Florence se déroule un concile chargé de travailler à la réunification des Églises d'Orient et d'Occident.	▮ In Florence vindt een concilie plaats, waarbij de unificatie van de Westelijke en de Oostelijk kerk wordt bediscussieerd.

1440-1493	▮ Frederick III of Habsburg reigned over the Holy Roman Empire.	▮ Friedrich III von Habsburg ist Kaiser des Heiligen Römischen Reiches.	▮ Frédéric III de Habsbourg, empereur du Saint Empire.	▮ Frederik III van het huis van Habsburg is keizer van het Heilige Roomse Rijk.
1441	▮ Jan van Eyck died.	▮ Jan van Eyck stirbt.	▮ Mort de Jan Van Eyck.	▮ Jan van Eyck overlijdt.
1443-1445	▮ Leon Battista Alberti wrote his treatise *De re aedificatoria*.	▮ Leon Battista Alberti schreibt *De re aedificatoria.*	▮ Leon Battista Alberti publie son *De re aedificatoria.*	▮ Leon Battista Alberti schrijft het *De re aedificatoria.*
1445	▮ Botticelli was born.	▮ Botticelli wird geboren.	▮ Naissance de Botticelli.	▮ Geboorte van Botticelli.
1449-1453	▮ Final phase of the Hundred Years War, begun in 1337.	▮ Letzte Phase des Hundertjährigen Krieges, angefangen im 1337.	▮ Dernière phase de la guerre de Cent ans, débutée en 1337.	▮ Laatse fase van de Honderdjarige Oorlog, begonnen in 1337.
1450	▮ Leon Battista Alberti designed the Malatesta Temple in Rimini.	▮ Leon Battista Alberti plant den Tempio Malatestiano von Rimini.	▮ Leon Battista Alberti dresse les plans du temple Malatesta de Rimini.	▮ Leon Battista Alberti ontwerpt de Tempio Malatestiano van Rimini.
1452	▮ Piero della Francesca began the *Legend of the True Cross* fresco cycle in the church of San Francesco in Arezzo. Leonardo da Vinci was born.	▮ Piero della Francesca beginn die Fresken mit den *Legenden des wahren Kreuzes* in der Kirche San Francesco von Arezzo. Leonardo da Vinci wird geboren.	▮ Piero della Francesca commence les fresques de la *Légende de la Vraie Croix* dans la basilique San Francesco d'Arezzo. Naissance de Léonard de Vinci.	▮ Piero della Francesca begint aan de fresco's met de *Legende van het Ware Kruis* in de San Francesco Kerk in Arezzo. Geboorte van Leonardo da Vinci.
1453	▮ Constantinople fell to the Muslims.	▮ Konstantinopel fällt durch die Hand der Osmanen.	▮ Prise de Constantinople par les Turcs ottomans.	▮ Constantinopel valt in handen van de Ottomanen.
1453-1485	▮ The Wars of the Roses were fought in England.	▮ In England kämpft man den Rosenkrieg.	▮ Guerre civile dite « des Deux-Roses » en Angleterre.	▮ In Engeland worden de Rozenoorlogen gevoerd.

c. 1455	Gutenberg invented the printing press with movable type.	Gutenberg hat den Druck mit beweglichen Lettern erfunden.	Gutenberg met au point l'impression typographique.	Uitvinding van de drukpers door Gutenberg.
1458	Matthias Corvinus was elected King of Hungary.	Matthias I Corvinus wird zum König von Ungarn ernannt.	Matthias Ier Corvin, roi de Hongrie.	Matthias Corvinus I wordt verkozen tot koning van Hongarije.
1458-1464	Papacy of Pius II.	Pontifikat von Pius II.	Pontificat de Pie II.	Het pontificaat van Pius II.
1461-1483	Louis XI of the house of Valois reigned in France.	In Frankreich herrscht Ludwig XI von Valois.	Louis XI de Valois, roi de France.	Lodewijk XI van Valois regeert in Frankrijk.
1465-1474	Andrea Mantegna painted the frescos of the *Bridal Chamber* of the Ducal Palace in Mantova.	Andrea Mantegna malt das Fresko in der *Camera degli Sposi* im Palazzo Ducale von Mantua.	Andrea Mantegna réalise le décor de fresques de la *Chambre des Époux*, au palais ducal de Mantoue.	Andrea Mantegna verwezenlijkt het fresco als decoratie van de *Camera degli Sposi* in het Palazzo Ducale van Mantua.
1469	Lorenzo il Magnifico succeeded his father Piero (the Gouty) in Florence. The marriage of Isabella of Castile and Ferdinand of Aragon united their kingdoms.	In Florenz ist Lorenzo der Prächtige der Nachfolger von Piero dem Gichtigen. Die Hochzeit zwischen Isabella von Kastilien und Ferdinand von Aragon vereint ihre beiden Reiche.	À Florence, Laurent le Magnifique succède à son père, Pierre le Goutteux. Mariage de Ferdinand d'Aragon et d'Isabelle de Castille, qui unissent leurs deux royaumes.	Lorenze *il Magnifico* volgt pater Piero 'de Jichtige' op in Florence. Huwelijk tussen Isabella van Castillië en Ferdinand van Aragon, die hiermee hun rijken verenigden.
1471	Dürer was born.	Dürer wird geboren.	Naissance de Dürer.	Geboorte van Dürer.
1471-1484	Papacy of Sixtus IV.	Pontifikat von Sixtus IV.	Pontificat de Sixte IV.	Het pontificaat van Sixtus IV.
1475	Michelangelo Buonarroti was born.	Michelangelo Buonarroti wird geboren.	Naissance de Michel-Ange Buonarroti.	Geboorte van Michelangelo Buonarroti.

1478	▮ Giorgione was born.	▮ Giorgione wird geboren.	▮ Naissance de Giorgione.	▮ Geboorte van Giorgione.
1483	▮ Charles VII was crowned in France. Raffaello was born.	▮ Karl VIII besteigt den Thron von Frankreich. Raffael wird geboren.	▮ Charles VIII monte sur le trône de France. Naissance de Raphaël.	▮ Karel VIII bestijgt de troon van Frankrijk. Geboorte van Rafaël.
1485-1509	▮ Henry VII, founder of the Tudor dynasty, reigned in England	▮ Heinrich VII herrscht über England, Begründer der Tudor-Dynastie.	▮ Henri VII, roi d'Angleterre et fondateur de la dynastie Tudor.	▮ Hendrik VII, stichter van de Tudor-dynastie, regeert in Engeland.
c. 1490	▮ Tiziano was born.	▮ Tizian wird geboren.	▮ Naissance de Titien.	▮ Geboorte van Titiaan.
1492	▮ Columbus discovered America. Lorenzo il Magnifico died.	▮ Kolumbus entdeckt den neuen Kontinent. Der Tod von Lorenzo dem Prächtigen.	▮ Christophe Colomb découvre le Nouveau Monde. Mort de Laurent le Magnifique.	▮ Columbus ontdekt het Nieuwe Continent. Lorenzo il Magnifico overlijdt.
1494	▮ Charles VIII of the house of Valois invaded Italy.	▮ Karl VIII. von Valois fällt in Italien ein.	▮ Charles VIII de Valois se lance dans les guerres d'Italie.	▮ Karel VIII van Valois treedt af in Italië.
1499-1501	▮ Amerigo Vespucci's expeditions to the New World.	▮ Entdeckungsreise in der Neuen Welt von Amerigo Vespucci.	▮ Expéditions d'Amerigo Vespucci dans le Nouveau Monde.	▮ Expeditie van Amerigo Vespucci naar het Nieuwe Continent.
1500	▮ Louis XII and Ferdinand the Catholic signed the Treaty of Granada to divide Italy.	▮ Abkommen von Granada über die Aufteilung Italiens zwischen Ludwig XII. und Ferdinand dem Katholischen.	▮ Le traité de Grenade partage l'Italie entre Louis XII et Ferdinand le Catholique.	▮ Verdrag van Granada voor de verdeling van Italië tussen Lodewijk XII en Ferdinand de Katholiek.
1501-1504	▮ Michelangelo sculpted the *David* in Firenze.	▮ Michelangelo meißelt den *David* in Florenz.	▮ Michel-Ange sculpte le *David* de Florence.	▮ Michelangelo houwt de *David* in Florence.
1503-1504	▮ Leonardo painted the *Mona Lisa* in Firenze.	▮ In Florenz malt Leonardo die *Mona Lisa*.	▮ Léonard de Vinci peint la *Joconde* à Florence.	▮ In Florence schildert Leonardo de *Mona Lisa*.

1503-1509	Papacy of Julius II.	Pontifikat von Julius II.	Pontificat de Jules II.	Het pontificaat van Julius II.
1508-1511	Raffaello painted the frescos in the *Stanza della Segnatura*.	Raffael malt die Fresken der *Stanza della Segnatura*.	Raphaël réalise les fresques de la *Chambre de la Signature*.	Rafaël brengt het fresco in de *Stanza della Segnatura* aan.
1508-1512	Michelangelo painted the frescos on the ceiling of the *Sistine Chapel*.	Michelangelo malt die Fresken des Gewölbes der *Sixtinischen Kapelle*.	Michel-Ange peint les fresques de la voûte de la *chapelle Sixtine*.	Michelangelo brengt het fresco op het gewelf van de *Sixtijnse Kapel* aan.
1509	Henry VIII ascended the throne of England.	Heinrich VIII besteigt den englischen Thron.	Henri VIII monte sur le trône d'Angleterre.	Hendrik VIII bestijgt de Engelse troon.
1511	Julius II sent the Holy League to war against Louis XII.	Julius II startet mit der Heiligen Liga gegen Ludwig XII.	Jules II réunit la Sainte Ligue contre Louis XII.	Julius II ordonneert de Heilige Liga tegen Lodewijk XII.
1513-1521	Papacy of Leo X.	Pontifikat von Leo X.	Pontificat de Léon X.	Het pontificaat van Leo X.
1517	Martin Luther nailed his 95 Theses to the door of the church in Wittemberg.	Martin Luther nagelt die 95 Thesen an die Tür der Schlosskirche zu Wittenberg.	Martin Luther affiche ses 95 thèses sur la porte de l'église du château de Wittenberg.	Maarten Luther bevestigt de 95 stellingen op de deur van de kerk van Wittenberg.
1519	Carlos I of Spain was elected emperor and took the name of Charles V. Leonardo died in Amboise.	Karl I von Spanien wird zum Kaiser mit dem Namen Karl V ernannt. Leonardo stirbt in Amboise.	Charles Ier d'Espagne devient empereur sous le nom de Charles Quint. Mort à Amboise de Léonard de Vinci.	Karel I van Spanje wordt gekozen tot keizer onder de naam Karel V. Leonardo overlijdt in Amboise.
1520	Leo X excommunicated Luther with the papal bull, *Exsurge Domine*. Raffaello died in Rome.	Leo X. exkommuniziert Luther mit der Bulle *Exsurge Domine*. Raffael stirbt in Rom.	Le pape Léon X excommunie Luther par la bulle *Exsurge Domine*. Mort à Rome de Raphaël.	Leo X excommuniceert Luther met de bul *Exsurge Domine*. Rafaël overlijdt in Rome.

1521	▮ Suleiman the Magnificent led the Ottomans to conquer Belgrade.	▮ Die Türken von Suleiman dem Prächtigen erobern Belgrad.	▮ Les Turcs de Soliman le Magnifique prennent Belgrade.	▮ De Turken van Süleyman de Grote veroveren Belgrado.
1526	▮ The Ottoman army of Suleiman the Magnificent defeated the Hungarians of Louis II. Jagiellon at Mohacs. François I lead the League of Cognac against Spain. The Diet of Speyer.	▮ In der Schlacht von Mohács unterliegen die Ungaren von Ludwig II Jagiellon den Türken von Suleiman dem Prächtigen. Franz I verwirklicht die Liga von Cognac gegen Spanien. Reichstag zu Speyer.	▮ Les Turcs de Soliman le Magnifique remportent la bataille de Mohács sur les Hongrois de Louis II Jagellon. François Ier réunit la ligue de Cognac contre l'Espagne. Diète de Spire.	▮ De Turken van Süleyman de Grote verslaan de Hongaren van Lodewijk II van het Huis Jagiello in Mohàcs. Liga van Cognac geordonneerd door Frans I tegen Spanje. Rijksdag van Spiers.
1527	▮ The lansquenets of Charles V sacked Rome.	▮ Plünderung Roms durch die Landsknechte von Karl V.	▮ Sac de Rome par les lansquenets de Charles Quint.	▮ Plundering van Rome door tussenkomst van de landsknechten van Karel V.
c. 1528	▮ Pieter Bruegel the Elder was born. Dürer died. Restructuring of the palace at Fontainebleau began.	▮ Pieter Bruegel der Ältere wird geboren. Dürer stirbt. Beginn der Restaurierung von Schloss Fontainbleau.	▮ Naissance de Pieter Bruegel l'Ancien. Mort du Dürer. Début du remaniement du château de Fontainebleau.	▮ Geboorte van Pieter Bruegel de Oude. Dürer overlijdt. Begin van de herstructurering van het Kasteel van Fontainebleau.
1529	▮ France and Spain signed the Treaty of Cambrai (or Peace of the Ladies).	▮ Friede von Cambrai (Damenfrieden) zwischen Frankreich und Spanien.	▮ Paix de Cambrai (paix des Dames) entre la France et l'Espagne.	De Damesvrede van Kamerijk tussen Frankrijk en Spanje.
1530	▮ In Bologna Tiziano did a portrait of Charles V, thus beginning his series of official portraits for the imperial court.	▮ In Bologna malt Tizian das Portrait von Karl V, und beginnt so seine Tätigkeit als Porträtmaler am kaiserlichen Hof.	▮ À Bologne, Titien peint un portrait de Charles V, inaugurant du même coup sa carrière de peintre de la cour impériale.	▮ Titiaan schildert in Bologne een portret van Karel V, het begin van zijn activiteiten als portrettist aan het keizerlijke hof.
1532	▮ Francisco Pizarro conquered the empire of the Incas.	▮ Die Eroberung des Inkareichs durch Francisco Pizarro.	▮ Francisco Pizarro conquiert l'Empire Inca.	▮ Francisco Pizarro verovert het Incarijk.

1533	Portuguese colonization of Brazil.	Portugiesische Kolonisierung von Brasilien.	Les Portugais colonisent le Brésil.	Portugese kolonisatie van Brazilië.
1534	The Act of Supremacy marked the birth of the Anglican Church.	Mit der Suprematsakte wird die anglikanische Kirche geboren.	L'Acte de suprématie consacre la naissance de l'Église anglicane.	De Act of Supremacy sancioneert de geboorte van de Anglicaanse Kerk.
1534-1549	Papacy of Paul III.	Pontifikat von Paul III.	Pontificat de Paul III.	Het pontificaat van Paulus III.
1537	Cosimo de' Medici became duke of Firenze.	Cosimo de' Medici wird Herzog von Florenz.	Côme de Médicis devient duc de Florence.	Cosimo de' Medici wordt Hertog van Florence.
1544	Pope Paul III convened the Council of Trent.	Einberufung des Konzils von Trient durch Paul III.	Le pape Paul III convoque le concile de Trente.	Paulus III roept de Concilie van Trente bijeen.
1555-1559	Papacy of Paul IV.	Pontifikat von Paul IV.	Pontificat de Paul IV.	Het pontificaat van Paulus IV.
1556	Charles V abdicated: Ferdinand I inherited the imperial throne and Habsburg possessions. Philip II became King of Spain and the Netherlands.	Abdankung von Karl V: Ferdinand I bekommt den Kaisertitel und alle dazugehörige Rechte. Philipp wird König von Spanien und den Niederländen.	Abdication de Charles V : Ferdinand Ier obtient le titre impérial et les possessions des Habsbourg. Philippe II devient roi d'Espagne et des Pays-Bas.	Troonsafstand van Karel V: Ferdinand I verkrijgt de keizerlijke titel en alle daarbij behorende rechten. Filips II werd koning van Spanje en Nederland.
1558	In England Elizabeth I, of the house of Tudor, succeeded Mary Stuart, a Catholic.	In England ist Elisabeth I Tudor die Nachfolgerin der katholischen Maria.	En Angleterre, Élisabeth Ire Tudor succède à Marie la Catholique.	Elizabeth I Tudor volgt Maria de Katholieke op.
1558-1583	Ivan IV warred against Sweden and Poland in the Baltic.	Lievländischer Krieg von Iwan IV gegen Schweden und Polen.	La guerre de Livonie oppose Ivan IV à la Suède et à la Pologne.	Lijflandse oorlog van Ivan IV tegen Zweden en Polen.
1559	The Peace of Cateau-Cambresis.	Frieden von Cateau-Cambresis.	Paix du Cateau-Cambrésis.	Vrede van Cateau-Cambrésis.

1560	▮ Vasari began construction of the Uffizi in Firenze.	▮ In Florenz beginnt Vasari an den Uffizien zu arbeiten.	▮ À Florence, Giorgio Vasari commence la construction des Offices.	▮ In Florence begint Vasari aan de werkzaamheden bij de Uffizi.
1564	▮ Michelangelo died.	▮ Michelangelo stirbt.	▮ Mort de Michel-Ange.	▮ Michelangelo overlijdt.
***c.* 1566**	▮ El Greco arrived in Venezia from Crete.	▮ El Greco reist von Kreta aus nach Venedig	▮ À Venise arrive, depuis la Crète, le Gréco.	▮ El Greco bereikt Venetië vanuit Kreta.
1569	▮ Pieter Bruegel died.	▮ Pieter Bruegel stirbt.	▮ Mort de Pieter Bruegel.	▮ Pieter Bruegel overlijdt.
1571	▮ Caravaggio was born in Milano.	▮ In Mailand wird Caravaggio geboren.	▮ Naissance à Milan de Caravage.	▮ Caravaggio wordt in Milaan geboren.
1576	▮ Tiziano died.	▮ Tizian stirbt.	▮ Mort de Titien.	▮ Titiaan overlijdt.
1580	▮ Philip II of Spain annexed Portugal. In Bologna Cardinal Gabriele Paleotti published his *Treatise on sacred and profane images*, the point of reference for the iconography of the Counter-Reformation.	▮ Philipp II von Spanien annektiert Portugal. Kardinal Gabriele Paleotti veröffentlicht in Bologna sein *Discorso intorno alle immagini sacre e profane*, ein Handbuch über die Ikonographie der Gegenreform.	▮ Philippe II d'Espagne annexe le Portugal. Le cardinal Gabriele Paleotti publie à Bologne le *De sacris et profanis imaginibus*, véritable précis d'iconographie de la Contre-Réforme.	▮ Filips II van Spanje annexeert Portugal. Kardinaal Gabriele Paleotti publiceert in Bologne het *Discorso intorno alle immagini sacre e profane*, handboek over de contrareformistische iconografie.
1589	▮ The murder of Henry III extinguished the house of Valois. Henry IV, of the house of Bourbon, ascended the throne of France.	▮ Ermordung von Heinrich III mit dem Erlöschen des Hauses Valois. Heinrich IV von Borbon besteigt den Thron von Frankreich.	▮ L'assassinat d'Henri III met fin à la dynastie des Valois. Henri IV de Bourbon monte sur le trône de France.	▮ Hendrik III vermoord, waardoor het Huis van Valois tot een einde kwam. Hendrik IV van Bourbon bestijgt de troon van Frankrijk.
1599	▮ Velázquez was born in Seville.	▮ In Sevilla wird Velázquez geboren.	▮ Naissance à Séville de Velásquez.	▮ Velázquez wordt in Sevilla geboren.

Biographies
Biografien
Biografieën

Leon Battista Alberti

Genova 1404 - Roma 1472

1420-1428 Bologna: Humanistic studies / Humanistische Studien / Suit des études humanistes / volgt een humanistische studie

1432 Roma

1434-1442 Firenze: studied Brunelleschi, Donatello and Masaccio / Er studiert Brunelleschi, Donatello und Masaccio / Étudie Brunelleschi, Donatello et Masaccio / Bestudeert Brunelleschi, Donatello en Masaccio

1435 *De Pictura*

1446-1451 Palazzo Rucellai, Firenze

c. 1450 Tempio Malatestiano, Rimini

1456-1470 Santa Maria Novella, Firenze: façade / Kirchenfassade / voorgevel van de kerk

1459 Mantova

c. 1460 San Sebastiano, Mantova

1467 Cappella Rucellai, Firenze

1472 Sant'Andrea, Mantova

Albrecht Altdorfer

Regensburg *c.* 1480 - 1538

1505 Regensburg

1506 Produced a series of copper engravings: considered the master of the Danube school / Ausführung einer Reihe von Kupferradierungen; er gilt als Meister der Donauschule / Réalise une série de gravures sur cuivre ; il est considéré comme le maître de l'École danubienne / Verwezenlijkt een serie van koperetsen; wordt overwogen als leraar aan de Donau School

1509-1516 *Saint Sebastian Altarpiece / Sebastianaltar / Retable de saint Sébastien / St. Sebastiaan Altaar* (Stiftsgalerie, San Florian-Linz)

1511 Travelled along the Danube, he was infl uenced by Dürer and cranach / Donaureise; steht unter dem Einfluss von Dürer und Cranach/ Voyage le long du Danube ; subit l'influence de Dürer et de Cranach/ Reis langs de Donau; wordt beïnvloed door Dürer en Cranach

1515-1516 *Crucifixion / Kreuzigung / Crucifixion / Kruisiging* (Gemäldegalerie, Kassel)

1528-1529 *The Battle of Issus / Die Alexanderschlacht / La Bataille d'Alexandre / Slag bij Issus* (Alte Pinakothek, München)

1530-1538 Deeply involved in the city government and as city architect / Er ist immer mehr in der Stadtverwaltung und als Stadtarchitekt tätig / Toujours plus engagé dans le gouvernement de sa ville, il en est aussi l'architecte officiel / Wijdt zich steeds meer aan het stadsbeheer en als stadsarchitect

1537 *Lot and His Daughters / Lot und seine Töchter / Loth et ses filles / Lot en zijn dochters* (Kunsthistorisches Museum, Wien)

Giuseppe Arcimboldo

Milano 1527 - 1593

1549 Working in his father's workshop/ Er lernt in der väterlichen Werkstatt / Travaille dans l'atelier paternel / Werkt in de werkplaats van zijn vader

1562 Wien: Began to paint for the imperial court, first at the service of Maximilian II and later of Rudolph II of Habsburg / Er beginnt am Kaiserhof zu malen, zuerst für Maximilian II., dann für Rudolf II. von Habsburg / Il commence à peindre pour la cour, d'abord au service de Maximilien II, puis à celui de Rodolphe II de Habsbourg / Begint met het schilderen voor het Keizerlijk Hof, eerst in dienst van Maximiliaan II, daarna voor Rudolf II van Habsburg

1563-1566 *The Four Seasons / Die Vier Jahreszeiten / Les Saisons / Allegorieën van de Seizoenen* (Kunsthistorisches Museum, Wien)

1566 *The Librarian and The Lawyer / Der Bibliothekar und Der Jurist / Le Bibliothécaire et l'Avocat / De Bibliothecaris en De Advocaat* (Skoklosters Slott, Stockholm)

1575 *Self Portrait / Selbstbildnis / Autoportrait / Zelfportret* (Naròdni Galerie, Prague)
1587 Milano
1590 *The Greengrocer / Der Gemüsegärtner / L'Homme-potager / De Groentenboer* (Museo Civico Ala Ponzone, Cremona)
1591 *Emperor Rudolph II as Vertumnus / Rudolph II. als Vertumnus / Rodolphe II en Vertumne / Rudolf II als Vertumnus* (Skoklosters Slott, Stockholm)

Hieronymus Bosch
s' Hertogenbosch *c.* 1450 - 1516

1470-1475 Lived and worked in his hometown / Er arbeitet in seiner Geburtsstadt / Exerce son activité dans sa ville natale / Voert zijn activiteiten uit in zijn geboortestad
1475-1480 *The Seven Deadly Sins / Die sieben Todsünden / Les Sept Péchés capitaux / De zeven hoofdzonden* (Museo del Prado, Madrid)
1484-1485 *Ecce Homo* (Städelsches Kunstinstitut, Frankfurt)
1490 *The Road to Calvary / Christus am Kalvarienberg / Cristo con la Cruz a cuestas / De (Weense) Kruisdraging* (Kunsthistorisches Museum, Wien)
1490-1500 *The Road to Calvary / Die Kreuzigungtragung / Montée au Calvaire / Kruisdraging* (Musée du Louvre, Paris)
1500-1504 Probably travelled in Italy / Wahrscheinliche Italienreise / Probable voyage en Italie / Reist vermoedelijk naar Italië
1503-1504 *Garden of Earthly Delights Triptych / Triptychon: Der Garten der Lüste / Triptyque du Jardin des Délices / Triptiek van de Tuin der Lusten* (Museo del Prado, Madrid)
1504 *The Last Judgement / Das Jüngste Gericht / Jugement Dernier / Het Laatste Oordeel* (Gemäldegalerie der Akademie, Wien)
1508-1509 *The Crowning with Thorns / Dornenkrönung Christi / Couronnement d'épines / De Doornenkroning van Christus* (National Gallery, London); *Adoration of the Magi Altarpiece / Triptychon: Anbetung der Heiligen Drei Könige / Triptyque de l'Adoration des Mages / Driekoningendrieluik* (Museo del Prado, Madrid)
1510-1516 *The Road to Calvary / Die Kreuztragung Christi / Portement de croix, avec sainte Véronique / De Kruisdraging* (Museum voor Schone Kunsten, Gent)

Sandro Botticelli
Firenze 1445 - 1510

1464-1467 Apprentice to Filippo Lippi and Verrocchio / Er ist Schüler von Filippo Lippi und Verrocchio / Élève de Filippo Lippi et de Verrocchio / Is leerling van Filippo Lippi en Verrocchio
1472 Listed among the painters who belonged to the Compagnia di San Luca / Er ist einer der eingeschriebenen Maler der Sankt-Lukas-Gilde / Figure parmi les peintres inscrits à la Compagnie de Saint-Luc / Behoort tot de schilders, die zijn ingeschreven bij het Sint-Lucasgilde
1477-1478 *Primavera* (Firenze, Galleria degli Uffizi)
c. 1481 Contributed to the decorations of the Cappella Sistina with Cosimo Rosselli, Domenico Ghirlandaio and Pietro Perugino / Mit Cosimo Rosselli, Domenico Ghirlandaio und Pietro Perugino nimmt er an der Dekoration der Sixtinischen Kapelle teil / Participe avec Cosimo Rosselli, Domenico Ghirlandaio et Pietro Perugino à la décoration de la chapelle Sixtine / Neemt met Cosimo Rosselli, Domenico Ghirlandaio en Pietro Perugino deel aan het decoreren van de Sixtijnse Kapel
1483-1485 *Birth of Venus / Geburt der Venus / Naissance de Vénus / Geboorte van Venus* (Galleria degli Uffizi, Firenze)
1485 *Bardi Altarpiece / Bardi Altar / Retable Bardi / Bardi-Altaarstuk* (Gemäldegalerie, Berlin)
1487 *Madonna of the Pomegranate / Madonna mit dem Granatapfel / Vierge à la Grenade / Madonna met de Granaatappel* (Galleria degli Uffizi, Firenze)
1491 A member of the committee called on to judge the projects to complete Arnolfi's façade for Santa Maria del Fiore / Er ist Mitglied der Kommission von Künstlern und Bürgern, die sich

zu den Projekten zur Fertigstellung der Arnolfo Fassade der Santa Maria del Fiore äußern soll / Fait partie de la commission d'artistes et de citoyens appelée à se prononcer sur les projets pour l'achèvement de la façade arnolfienne de Santa Maria del Fiore / Maakt deel uit van een commissie van kunstenaars en staatsburgers, opgeroepen om zich uit te spreken over het project voor het completeren van de Arnolfo-voorgevel van de Santa Maria del Fiore

c. 1495 Under the influence of Savonarola's preaching he began to paint mystical subjects / Unter dem Einfluss der Predigten von Savonarola beginnt er Werke mystischen Charakters zu malen / Sous l'influence de la prédication de Savonarole, il commence à peindre des œuvres à caractère mystique / Begint, beïnvloedt door de preek van Savonarola, met het schilderen van werken met een mystiek karakter

1496-1497 *Lamentation over the Dead Christ / Beweinung Christi / Déploration sur le Christ mort / Bewening van Christus* (Alte Pinakothek, München)

1501 *Mystic Natività / Anbetung der Heiligen Drei Könige / Nativité mystique / Mystieke Geboorte* (National Gallery, London)

Donato Bramante

Fermignano, Pesaro 1444 - Roma 1514

1477 Bergamo, Palazzo del Podestà: Frescoed the façade / Fresko an der Fassade / Peint à fresque la façade / Fresco op de voorgevel

1478 Milano

1482-1486 Santa Maria presso San Satiro

1488 Collaborated with other architects on reconstruction of the cathedral of Pavia and participated in the debate about construction of the lantern for the cathedral in Milano / Mit anderen Architekten arbeitet er am Wiederaufbau des Doms in Pavia; er wird in die Debatte um den Bau des Tiburio des Mailänder Doms miteinbezogen / Intervient, avec d'autres architectes, dans la reconstruction du dôme de Pavie ; il est impliqué dans le débat sur la construction de la tour-lanterne du Dôme de Milan / Werkt samen met andere architecten aan de reconstructie van de Dom van Pavia; raakt betrokken bij het debat over de bouw van de vieringtoren van de Dom van Milaan

1492-1497 Began two projects: reconstruction of Santa Maria delle Grazie and the urban design for the square in Vigevano / Er beginnt mit zwei Projekten: dem Wiederaufbau der Kirche Santa Maria delle Grazie und der urbanistischen Definition der Piazza in Vigevano / Lance deux projets : la reconstruction de Santa Maria delle Grazie et la structuration de la place de Vigevano / Start twee projecten: de reconstructie van de Santa Maria delle Grazie en de stedenbouwkundige definitie van het plein van Vigevano

1499 Left Milano, invaded by French troups / Er verlässt das von den französischen Truppen besetzte Mailand / Quitte Milan envahie par les troupes françaises / Verlaat het door de Franse troepen bezette Milaan

1500 Roma

1500-1504 Santa Maria della Pace, Roma: Cloister and convent / Kreuzgang und Kloster / Cloître et couvent / Kloostergang en klooster

1502-1507 Tempietto di San Pietro in Montorio, Roma

1505 Began construction of the Belvedere courtyard for Pope Julius II and began design of the new San Pietro, which involved him until his death / Er beginnt für Julius II. den Bau des Gartens im Belvedere. Im gleichen Jahr beginnt er mit der Planung des neuen Petersdoms, was ihn bis zu seinem Tod beschäftigen wird / Commence pour Jules II la construction de la cour du Belvédère. Commence cette même année la conception du nouveau Saint-Pierre, qui l'occupera jusqu'à sa mort / Begint voor Paus Julius II aan de bouw van het hof van Belvedere. Begint in ditzelfde jaar aan het ontwerp van de nieuwe Sint-Pieter, waarmee hij zich tot aan zijn dood bezig hield

---

Pieter Bruegel de Oude
Breda 1528/30 - Bruxelles 1569

1545 Bruxelles: apprenticed to Pieter Coecke, who introduced him to the painting of Bosch / Er ist Schüler von Pieter Coecke, der ihn an die Malerei Boschs annähert / Est l'élève de Pieter Coecke, qui l'initie à la peinture de Bosch / Is leerling van Pieter Coecke, die met zijn schilderkunst in de buurt komt van Bosch

1551 A member of the guild of Saint Luke / Er tritt der Lukas-Gilde bei / Est inscrit à la Guilde de Saint-Luc / Is ingeschreven bij het Sint-Lucasgilde

c. 1552 Travelled in Italy / Italienreise / Voyage en Italie / Reist naar Italië

1558-1559 Developed a very original vision of a visionary and fantastic world in a series of paintings / Er malt eine Reihe von Bildern, in denen er außerordentlich originell eine phantastische und visionäre Welt entwickelt / Réalise une série de tableaux où il développe avec une grande originalité son univers fantastique et visionnaire / Voert een serie schilderijen uit, waarin hij buitengewoon origineel een fantastische en visionaire wereld creëert

1562 Amsterdam, Besançon, Amberes. Married Mayeken coecke, daughter of his master / Er heiratet Mayeken Coecke, die Tochter seines Meisters / Épouse Mayeken Coecke, la fille de son maître / Trouwt met Mayeken Coecke, dochter van zijn meester

1562-1567 Bruxelles: Painted religious subjects / Er malt Bilder mit religiösen Inhalten / Peint des œuvres à sujet religieux / Schildert werken met religieuze onderwerpen

1563 *The Tower of Babel / Turmbau zu Babel / La Tour de Babel / Toren van Babel* (Kunsthistoriches Museum, Wien)

Filippo Brunelleschi
Firenze 1377 - 1446

1398 Applied for membership in the guild of silk weavers (Arte della Seta), which accepted him in 1404 / Er bittet um die Aufnahme in die Seidenweberzunft und tritt 1404 bei / Demande son immatriculation à l'Arte della Seta (Guilde de la Soie) qui l'admettra en 1404 / Verzoekt om te worden ingeschreven bij de Arte della Seta, waar hij in 1404 zou worden toegelaten

1401 Competition for the Baptistery doors in Firenze: *Sacrifice of Isaac* / Wettbewerb um die Pforte des Baptisteriums in Florenz: *Das Opfer Isaaks* / Concours pour la porte du Baptistère de Florence: *Le Sacrifice d'Isaac* / Wedstrijd voor de deuren van het Baptisterium van Florence: *Offer van Isaac* (Museo Nazionale del Bargello, Firenze)

1402-1404 Roma: A visit to study the classics / Reise, um die Klassiker zu studieren / Voyage pour étudier le classicisme antique / Reis, voor het bestuderen van de Klassieken

1417 Firenze: First project for the dome of the cathedral / Erste Hypothese für die Kuppel des Doms / Premier projet pour la coupole du Dôme / Eerste hypothese voor de koepel van de Dom

1418 Won, together with Lorenzo Ghiberti, the competition for the dome of the cathedral / Er gewinnt mit Lorenzo Ghiberti den Wettbewerb um die Domkuppel / Remporte avec Lorenzo Ghiberti le concours pour la coupole du Dôme / Wint met Lorenzo Ghiberti de wedstrijd voor de koepel van de Dom

1418-1427 Ospedale degli Innocenti, Firenze

1420 Santa Maria del Fiore, Firenze: Works on the great dome began / Beginn der Bauarbeiten an der Kuppel / Début des travaux de la coupole / Begint met de werkzaamheden van de koepel

1421-1428 Sagrestia Vecchia, San Lorenzo, Firenze

1429-1444 Cappella Pazzi, Firenze

1444-1446 Santo Spirito, Firenze

Lucas Cranach
Kronach 1472 - Weimar 1553

1498 Left his father's workshop / Er verlässt die väterliche Werkstatt / Quitte l'atelier paternel / Verlaat de werkplaats van zijn vader. Wien

1500-1504 *Rest on the Flight to Egypt / Ruhe auf der Flucht / Le Repos pendant la fuite en Égypte / Rust op de vlucht naar Egypte* (Staatliche Museen, Berlin)

1505-1506 Wittenberg: Became an official artist of the Elector of Saxony. Also decorated the hunting castles / Er wird Hofmaler beim Kurfürsten von Sachsen. Darüber hinaus dekoriert er die Jagdschlösser / Devient le peintre officiel de l'Électeur de Saxe. Décore par ailleurs les rendez-vous de chasse / Wordt schilder van de Keurvorsten van Saksen. Decoreerde daarnaast de jachtkastelen (Koburg, Lochau, Thurgau)

1525 Joined the reformation of Luther / Er tritt der Reform Luthers bei / Adhère à la Réforme luthérienne / Sluit zich aan bij de Lutherse Reformatie

1529 *Portrait of Martin Luther / Portrait von Martin Luther / Portrait de Martin Luther / Portret van Maarten Luther* (Galleria degli Uffizi, Firenze)

1530 *The Paradise / Das Goldene Zeitalter / Le Paradis terrestre / Het Paradijs* (Kunsthistorisches Museum, Wien)

1531 *Venus and Cupid / Venus und Amor / Vénus et Cupidon / Venus en Cupido* (Galleria Borghese, Roma)

1546 *Fountain of Youth / Der Jungbrunnen / La Fontaine de jouvence / Fontein der Jeugd* (Staatliche Museen, Berlin)

1552 Weimar

Donatello
Firenze 1386 - 1466

1404-1407 Collaborated with Ghiberti on the north Doors of the Baptistery / Er arbeitet mit Ghiberti an der Nordpforte des Baptisteriums / Travaille avec Ghiberti à la porte Nord du Baptistère / Werkt met Ghiberti aan de noordelijke deur van het Baptisterium

1408 *David* (Museo Nazionale del Bargello, Firenze)

1409-1411 *San Giovanni Evangelista* (Museo dell'Opera del Duomo, Firenze)

1411-1412 *San Marco* (Museo di Orsammichele, Firenze)

1415-1435 *Prophets* for the belltower / *Die Propheten* für den Campanile / *Prophètes* pour le campanile / *Profeten* voor Klokkentoren

c. 1417 *San Giorgio* (Museo Nazionale del Bargello, Firenze)

1423-1427 *Feast of Herod* for the baptismal font / *Das Gastmahl des Herodes* für das Taufbecken / *Festin d'Hérode* pour les fonts baptismaux / *Banket van Herodes* voor het doopvont (Siena, Battistero)

1431-1433 Roma: *Tabernacle of the Sacrament / Tabernakel für das Sakrament / Tabernacle du Saint-Sacrement / Tabernakel voor het Sacrament*

1433-1439 Firenze: *Choir-stall* for the Florentine cathedral, stucco decorations and bronze doors for the old sacristy / *Cantoria* für den Florentiner Dom, Stuckdekoration und Bronzetüren für die Alte Sakristei / *Tribune des chantres* pour la cathédrale, décorations en stuc et portes en bronze pour l'Ancienne Sacristie / *Cantoria* voor de Florentijnse Kathedraal, decoraties van pleister en deuren van brons voor de Sagrestia Vecchia (Oude Sacristie)

c. 1440 Bronze *David* / *David* Bronze / *David* en bronze / Bronzen *David* (Museo Nazionale del Bargello, Firenze)

1443-1453 Padova: *Equestrian monument for Gattamelata*, bronze *Crucifix* and sculpted altarpiece for the high altar of the basilica of Sant'Antonio / *Reiterstandbild Gattamelata*, *Kruzifix* Bronze und bildhauerische Altartafel für die Basilika Sant'Antonio / *Monument équestre du Gattamelata*; *Crucifix* en bronze et Retable sculpté pour le grand autel de la basilique Saint-Antoine / *Ruiterstandbeeld van Gattamelata*, bronzen *Kruisiging* en gebeeldhouwd altaarstuk voor het grote altaar van de Sant'Antonio Basiliek

1457-1461 Siena: *The Baptist* in bronze (cathedral) / *Johannes der Täufer* in Bronze (Dom) / *Saint Jean-Baptiste* en bronze (cathédrale) / *Johannes de Doper* van brons (Kathedraal)

Albrecht Dürer
Nürnberg 1471 - 1528

1484 First *Self Portrait* / Erstes *Selbstbildnis* / Premier *Autoportrait* / Eerste *Zelfportret* (Graphische Sammlung Albertina, Wien)

1486 Apprenticed to Wolgemut and Pleydenwurff / Er wird ein Schüler von Wolgemut und Pleydenwurff / Élève de Wolgemut et de Pleydenwurff / Is leerling van Wolgemut en Pleydenwurff

1489-1490 Travelled in Europe and Italy / Reisen in Europa und Italien / Voyages en Europe et en Italie / Reist naar Europa en Italië

1490 *Portrait of Dürer's Father and Portrait of Dürer's Mother / Bildnis des Vaters und Bildnis der Mutter / Portrait de son père et Portrait de sa mère / Portret van zijn vader* (Galleria degli Uffizi, Firenze) en *Portret van zijn moeder* (Germanisches Nationalmuseum, Nürnberg)

1493 Basel: *Self Portrait with Eryngium Flower / Selbstbildnis mit Blume / Portrait de l'artiste tenant une fleur de chardon ou Autoportrait / Zelfportret met distel* (Musée du Louvre, Paris)

1494 *The Wire-Drawing Mill / Die Mühle / Le Moulin / De molen* (Staatliche Museen, Berlin)

1495 Began to specialise in engraving / Er beginnt sich mit Radierungen zu beschäftigen / Commence à se consacrer aux gravures / Begint zich toe te wijden aan het graveren

1497-1510 Woodcuts for the *Passion of Christ* / Radierungen für die *Große Passion Christi* / Gravures pour la *Grande Passion* / Gravures voor de *Grote Passie van Christus*

1498 *Paumgartner altarpiece / Paumgartner Altar / Retable Paumgartner / Paumgartner-altaar* (Alte Pinakothek, München)

1505 Second visit to Italy / Zweite Italienreise / Second voyage en Italie / Tweede reis naar Italië

1507 *Adam and Eve / Adam und Eva / Adam et Ève / Adam en Eva* (Museo del Prado, Madrid)

1511 *Adoration of the Holy Trinity / Anbetung der Trinität / Adoration de la Sainte Trinità / Aanbidding der Wijzen* (Kunsthistorisches Museum, Wien)

1512 Became the court painter of Maximilian I / Er wird Hofmaler bei Maximilian I/ Devient peintre de cour de Maxililien Ier/ Wordt hofschilder van Maximiliaan I

1521-1526 Painted the masterpieces of his mature years, portraits and religious subjects / Er arbeitet an seinen reifen Meisterwerken, an Bildnissen und Bildern religiösen Inhalts / Réalise les chefs-d'œuvre de sa maturité, portraits et tableaux à sujets religieux / Verwezenlijkt zijn rijpe meesterwerken, portretten en religieuze schilderijen

1526 *Madonna of the Pear / Maria mit Kind und mit der Birne / Vierge à l'Enfant tenant une poire / Maria en Kind, met peer* (Galleria degli Uffizi, Firenze)

Jean Fouquet
Tours c. 1425 - c. 1480

1444-1446 Travelled in Italy / Italienreise / Voyages en Italie / Reist in Italië: Napoli, Firenze, Ferrara

1445-1450 Returned to France, took on many commissions at the court in Paris and created works for the most powerful personages / Wieder in der Heimat, übernimmt er zahlreiche Aufträge am Pariser Hof und realisiert Werke für die ansehnlichsten Persönlichkeiten dort / De retour en France, assume de nombreuses charges à la cour et réalise des œuvres pour les plus puissants personnages / Keert terug naar zijn geboorteland, neemt talrijke opdrachten aan van het Parijse hof en verwezenlijkt werken bestemd voor de invloedrijkste personen

c. 1450 *Portrait of Charles VII / Portrait des Karl VII / Portrait de Charles VII / Portret van Karel VII* (Musée du Louvre, Paris); *The Melun Diptych / Diptychon von Melun / Diptyque de Melun / Diptiek van Melun* (Koninklijk Museum voor Schone Kunsten, Antwerpen; Staatliche Museen, Berlin)

1450-1455 Miniatures for the *Book of Hours of Etienne Chevalier* / Miniaturen für das *Stundenbuch von Etienne Chevalier* / Miniatures pour le *Livre d'Heures d'Étienne Chevalier* / Miniaturen voor het *Getijdenboek van Etienne Chevalier*

1460-1465 *Pietà* (Église de Nouans-Les-Fountaines)

1465 *Portrait of Guillaume Jouvenel des Ursins / Bildnis von Guillaume Jouvenel des Ursins / Portrait de Guillaume Jouvenel des Ursins / Portret van Guillaume Jouvenel des Ursins* (Musée du Louvre, Paris)

Giorgione

Castelfranco Veneto 1477/78 - Venezia 1510

c. 1485 Venezia: apprenticed to Giovanni Bellini / Er wird Schüler von Giovanni Bellini / Il est l'élève de Giovanni Bellini / Is leerling van Giovanni Bellini

c. 1500 Probably met Leonardo / Er begegnet wahrscheinlich Leonardo / Rencontre probable avec Léonard de Vinci / Ontmoet vermoedelijk Leonardo

1502 *Castelfranco Altarpiece / Castelfranco Altartafel / Retable de Castelfranco / Altaarstuk van Castelfranco* (Duomo, Castelfranco Veneto)

1502-1508 Painted some of his greatest masterpieces, full of allegorical significance that is often ambiguous or difficult to interpret / Einige seiner wichtigsten Meisterwerke, Werke mit allegorischem, oft mehrdeutigem oder schwer lesbarem Hintergrund / Exécute quelques-uns de ses plus grands chefs-d'œuvre, œuvres à la signification allégorique souvent ambiguë ou de lecture difficile / Verwezenlijkt twee grote meesterwerken, werken van allegorische waarde, vaak dubbelzinnig of moeilijk te lezen

1507-1508 *The Tempest / Das Gewitter / La Tempête / La Tempesta (Het Onweer)* (Venezia, Gallerie dell'Accademia)

c. 1508 *The Three Philosophers / Die Drei Philosophen / Les Trois philosophes / Drie Filosofen* (Kunsthistorisches Museum, Wien)

1508 Venezia, Fondaco de' Tedeschi: Collaborated with Tiziano on the frescos / Er arbeitet mit Tizian an den Fresken / Collabore avec Titien aux fresques / Werkt samen met Titiaan aan de fresco's

1508-1510 *Sleeping Venus / Schlummernde Venus / Vénus enormie / Slapende Venus* (Gemäldegalerie Alte Meister, Dresden)

Matthias Grünewald

Würzburg c. 1480 - Halle 1528

1504-1505 Painted the earliest work attributed to him with certainty: *Mocking of Christ* / Erstes gesichertes Werk: *Die Verspottung Christi* / Exécute sa première œuvre certaine, *Le Christ aux outrages* / Verwezenlijkt zijn eerste verzekerde werk: *Bespotting van Christus* (Alte Pinakothek, München)

1510 Mainz: Worked as a hydraulic engineer and at the service of the archbishop Uriel von gemmingen / Er arbeitet als Wasserkunstmacher im Dienste des Erzbischofs Uriel von Gemmingen / Travaille comme ingénieur hydraulicien, au service du prince-archevêque Uriel von Gemmingen / Werkt als hydraulisch ingenieur en is in dienst van de aartsbisschop Uriel von Gemmingen

1512-1515 Large polyptych for the church of the convent of St. Anthony in Isenheim / Großes Polyptychon für die Klosterkirche der Antoniten in Isenheim / Grand polyptyque pour l'église du couvent des Antonins, à Issenheim / Groot veelluik voor de kerk van het Sant'Antonio Klooster in Isenheim

1516 Mainz

1523-1525 *Deposition of Christ / Die Beweinung Christi / Déposition du Christ / Bewening van Christus* (Colegiata de Aschaffenburg)

1525-1526 *Way to Calvary and Crucifixion / Kreuztragung und Kreuzigung / Montée au Calvaire et Crucifixion / Kruisdraging en Kruisiging* (Staatliche Kunsthalle, Karlsruhe)

1526 Exiled from the city because suspected of being a lutheran / Er steht im Verdacht Lutheraner zu sein und muss die Stadt verlassen / Soupçonné de luthéranisme, il est éloigné de la ville / Wordt er van verdacht Lutheraan te zijn en wordt de stad uit gestuurd

---

Hans Holbein der Jüngere
Augsburg 1497/98 - London 1543

1515 Basel: Son of Hans the Elder, began his apprenticeship in his father's workshop / Als Sohn von Hans dem Älteren beginnt er in der väterlichen Werkstatt zu lernen / Fils de Hans l'Ancien, il commence son apprentissage dans l'atelier paternel / Begint zijn scholing als zoon van Hans de Oude, bij de werkplaats van zijn vader

1517-1519 First visit to Italy / Erste Italienreise / Premier voyage en Italie / Eerste reis naar Italië

1522 *Gerster Altarpiece / Gerster Altar / Retable Gerster / Gerster Altaarstuk* (Museum der Stadt, Solothurn)

1526 *Meyer Madonna / Madonna des Bürgermeisters Meyer / Vierge avec la famille du bourgmestre Meyer / Madonna van burgemeester Meyer* (Hessen Collection, Darmstadt)

1526-1528 England / Angleterre / Engeland

1527 *Sir Thomas More* (Frick Collection, New York)

1529 *Portrait of the Artist's Wife and Children / Bildnis seiner Frau und seiner beiden Kinder / La Femme du peintre et ses enfants / Portret van zijn vrouw en zijn twee kinderen* (Kunstmuseum, Basel)

1530-1531 Second visit to Italy / Zweite Italienreise / Second voyage en Italie / Tweede reis naar Italië

1532 England / Angleterre / Engeland

1532-1533 *Georg Gisze* (Gemäldegalerie, Berlin); *The Ambassadors / Die Gesandten / Les Ambassadeurs / De Ambassadeurs* (National Gallery, London)

1536 Henry VIII nominated him the court painter / Heinrich VIII. ernennt ihn zum Hofmaler / Henri VIII le nomme peintre de la cour / Hendrik VIII benoemt hem tot Hofschilder

1536-1537 *Portrait of Jane Seymour / Bildnis der Jane Seymour / Portrait de Jane Seymour / Portret van Jane Seymour* (Kunsthistorisches Museum, Wien)

1540 *Portrait of Henry VIII / Bildnis des Königs Heinrich VIII / Portrait d'Henri VIII / Portret van Hendrik VIII* (Galleria Nazionale di Arte Antica di Palazzo Barberini, Roma)

Leonardo da Vinci
Vinci, Firenze 1452 - Amboise 1519

1469 Firenze: Apprentice in Verrocchio's workshop / Er arbeitet in der Werkstatt von Verrocchio / Travaille dans l'atelier de Verrocchio / Werkt in de werkplaats van Verrocchio

1478 Received his first independent commission: the altarpiece for the chapel of San Bernardo in Palazzo Vecchio / Er erhält seinen ersten selbständigen Auftrag: das Altarbild der Kapelle San Bernardo im Palazzo Vecchio / Reçoit sa première commande indépendante : le retable pour la chapelle San Bernardo dans le Palazzo Vecchio / Ontvangt zijn eerste onafhankelijke opdracht: het altaarstuk voor het altaar van de San Bernardo Kapel in het Palazzo Vecchio

1481 Received a commission from the monks at san Donato a Scopeto to paint an *Adoration of the Magi*, which remained unfinished / Er erhält von den Mönchen von San Donato in Scopeto den Auftrag, eine *Anbetung der Könige* zu malen, die aber unvollendet bleibt / Reçoit des moines de San Donato à Scopeto la commande d'une *Adoration des Mages* qui restera inachevée / Krijgt van de Monniken van San Donato de opdracht om een *Aanbidding der Wijzen* te schilderen, die onvoltooid blijft (Galleria degli Uffizi, Firenze)

1482 Milano

c. 1487 Castello Sforzesco: Designed the decorations / Er plant die Dekoration / Conçoit les décorations / Ontwerpt de decoraties

1488-1490 *Lady with an Ermine / Dame mit dem Hermelin / La Dame à l'hermine / De Dame met de Hermelijn* (Muzeum Czartoryski, Kraków)

1494-1498 *Last Supper / Das Letzte Abendmahl / Cène / Laatste Avondmaal* (Santa Maria delle Grazie, Milano)

1501 Cartoon for *Madonna and Child with St. Anne and young St. John* / Karton der *Hl. Anna, der Madonna, dem Kind und Johannes des Täufers* / Carton pour *La Vierge à l'Enfant, avec sainte Anne et saint Jean-Baptiste* / Karton voor *Sint-Anna, de Madonna, het Kind en*

Johannes de Doper (National Gallery, London)

1502-1503 In the entourage of Cesare Borgia / Am Hofe des Cesare Borgia / Il est dans la suite de César Borgia / Behoort tot het gevolg van Cesare Borgia

1503 Firenze, Palazzo Vecchio: *The Battle of Anghiari / Die Schlacht von Anghiari / La Bataille d'Anghiari / Slag bij Anghiari*

1503-1506 *Mona Lisa / La Joconde* (Musée du Louvre, Paris)

1508-1513 *Madonna and Child with St. Anne / Maria mit dem Kind und Hl. Anna / La Vierge à l'Enfant avec sainte Anne / Madonna met Kind en Sint Anna-te-drieën* (Musée du Louvre, Paris)

1510 Milano: Began studying anatomy / Er beginnt mit seinen anatomischen Studien / Commence des études d'anatomie à Milan / Begint in Milaan met het bestuderen van de anatomie

1513-1516 *St. John the Baptist / Johannes der Täufer / Saint Jean-Baptiste / Johannes de Doper* (Musée du Louvre, Paris)

1517 Invited to France as a guest of François I / Er wird nach Frankreich an den Hof Franz I. eingeladen / François Ier l'accueille en France / Wordt naar Frankrijk geroepen als gast van Frans I

Andrea Mantegna

Isola di Carturo, Padova 1431 - Mantova 1506

1447 Venezia: Apprenticed to Squarcione / Schüler von Squarcione / Il est l'élève du Squarcione / Is leerling van Squarciane

1448 Padova: Commissioned, together with nicolò Pizzolo, to decorate the Ovetari chapel in the church of the Eremitani / Mit Nicolò Pizzolo erhält er de Auftrag, die Kapelle Ovetari in der Kirche der Eremitani zu schmücken / Reçoit avec Nicolò Pizzolo la commande de la décoration de la chapelle Ovetari, dans l'église des Eremitani / Ontvangt samen met Nicolò Pizzolo de opdracht voor het decoreren van de Ovetari Kapel in de Kerk van de Eremitani

1449 Ferrara

1452 Padova

1453 Married the daughter of Jacopo Bellini / Er heiratet die Tochter von Jacopo Bellini / Épouse la fille de Jacopo Bellini / Trouwt met de dochter van Jacopo Bellini; *St Luke Altarpiece / Altarbild San Luca / Retable de Saint-Luc / Altaarstuk van San Luca* (Pinacoteca di Brera, Milano)

1456-1459 *San Zeno Altarpiece / Altarbild San Zeno / Retable de San Zeno / Altaarstuk van San Zeno* (San Zeno, Verona)

1460 Mantova

1465-1474 Painted the *Bridal Chamber / Camera degli Sposi oder Camera Picta / Chambre des Époux / Bruidskamer* (Palazzo Ducale, Mantova)

1466 Visit to Toscana / Reise in die Toskana / Voyage en Toscane / Reist naar Toscane

1480 *St. Sebastian / Hl. Sebastian / Saint Sébastien / Heilige Sebastiaan* (Musée du Louvre, Paris)

c. 1483 *Dead Christ / Beweinung Christi / Le Christ mort / Dode Christus* (Pinacoteca di Brera, Milano)

1488-1490 Brief stay in Rome / Kurzer Romaufenthalt / Bref séjour à Rome / Kort verblijf in Rome

1497 *Madonna Trivulzio* (Museo d'Arte Antica del Castello Sforzesco, Milano)

Masaccio

San Giovanni Valdarno, Arezzo 1401 - Roma 1428

1417 Firenze: Apprentice / Lehrling / Apprentissage / Is Leerjongen

1420-1422 *St. Juvenal Triptych / Triptychon von San Giovenale / Triptyque de saint Juvénal / Triptiek van San Giovenale* (Pieve dei Santi Pietro e Paolo, Cascia)

1424 Firenze: Began the frescos of the Brancacci chapel with Masolino / Er beginnt mit Masolino die Dekoration der Kapelle Brancacci / Commence avec Masolino la décoration à fresque de la chapelle Brancacci / Begint met Masolino aan het decoreren van de Brancacci Kapel; *Madonna and Child with St. Anne / Sant'Anna Metterza / Sainte Anne Trinitarie / Sint Anna-te-drieën* (Galleria degli Uffizi, Firenze)

1425 Established his own workshop / Er eröffnet seine eigene Werkstatt / Ouvre son propre atelier / Richt zijn eigen werkplaats op

1426 *Pisa Polyptych* (today conserved in 5 different museums) / *Polyptychon von Pisa* (heute in 5 verschiedenen Museen aufbewahrt) / *Polyptyque de Pise* (conservé aujourd'hui dans cinq musées différents) / *Veelluik van Pisa* (tegenwoordig bewaard in 5 verschillende musea)

1426-1428 *The Holy Trinity / Trinità / Trinité / De Heilige Drieëenheid* (Santa Maria Novella, Firenze)

1428 Travelled to Roma where he died suddenly / Er begibt sich nach Rom, wo er plötzlich stirbt / Il se rend à Rome où il meurt brutalement / Begeeft zich naar Rome, waar hij plotseling overlijdt

---

Michelangelo Buonarroti

Caprese, Arezzo 1475 - Roma 1564

1490 Firenze: Studied in the convent garden of San Marco / Besucht er den Garten von San Marco / Fréquente le « Jardin de Saint-Marc » / Bezoekt de Giardino di San Marco

1492 *Madonna of the Stairs* and *Battle of the Centaurs* / *Madonna an der Treppe* und *Die Kentaurenschlacht* / La *Vierge à l'escalier* et le *Combat des centaures* / *Madonna van de Trappen* en het *Centaurengevecht* (Casa Buonarroti, Firenze)

1494 Sculpted an *Angel Candle-bearer*, *St. Proculus* and *St. Petronius* to complete the arch of San Domenico / Er meißelt zur Fertigstellung der Arca di San Domenico einen *Leuchterengel* und die Statuen der *Heiligen Prokulus* und *Petronius* / Sculpte, pour compléter le tombeau de saint Dominique, un *Ange* et les statues de *Saint Proculus* et *Saint Patrone* / Beeldhouwt, om de Arca di San Domenico af te maken, een *Engel met Kandelaar* en standbeelden van de Heiligen *Proculus* en *Petronius*

1496 Roma

1498-1499 *Pietà* (San Pietro, Città del Vaticano)

1501-1504 *David* (Galleria dell'Accademia, Firenze)

1504-1506 *Tondo Doni* (Galleria degli Uffizi, Firenze); *The Battle of Cascina / Schlacht von Cascina / Bataille de Cascina / De Slag bij Cascina* (Palazzo Vecchio, Firenze)

1505-1508 Roma: Summoned by JuliusII / Er wird zu Julius II. gerufen / Il est appelé par Jules II / Wordt opgeroepen door Julius II

1508-1512 Painted the ceiling of the Cappella Sistina / Er malt das Gewölbe der Sixtinischen Kapelle / Peint la voûte de la chapelle Sixtine / Beschildert het gewelf van de Sixtijnse Kapel

c. 1515 *Moses* for the tomb of Julius II / *Moses* für das Grabmal Julius II. / *Moïse* pour le tombeau de Jules II / *Mozes* voor de graftombe van Julius II (San Pietro in Vinicoli, Roma)

1515-1519 Firenze: Designed the façade of the church of San Lorenzo / Er entwirft die Fassade der Kirche San Lorenzo / Projet de la façade de l'église San Lorenzo / Ontwerpt de voorgevel van de Kerk van San Lorenzo

1520-1534 Sagrestia Nuova, San Lorenzo

1524-1534 Biblioteca Medicea Laurenziana

1534 Roma

1534-1541 *Last Judgement* in the Cappella Sistina / *Das Jüngste Gericht* in der Sixtinischen Kapelle / *Jugement Dernier* dans la chapelle Sixtine / *Het Laatste Oordeel* in de Sixtijnse Kapel

1546-1549 Began work on the project for the dome of San Pietro and oversaw completion of Palazzo Farnese / Beginn der Entwürfe für die Kuppel des Petersdoms und Leitung der Abschlussarbeiten des Palazzo Farnese / Commence la conception de la coupole de Saint-Pierre et surveille l'achèvement du palais Farnèse / Begint met het ontwerpen van de koepel van de Sint-Pieter en houdt toezicht op de voltooiing van het Palazzo Farnese

1550 Completed the frescos in the Cappella Paolina / Er beendet die Fresken in der Cappella Paolina / Termine les fresques de la chapelle Paolina / Voltooit de fresco's van de Paolina Kapel

1550-1555 *Pietà* for his own tomb / *Pietà* für das eigene Grabmal / *Pietà* pour son propre tombeau / *Pietà* voor zijn eigen graf (Museo dell'Opera del Duomo, Firenze)

1552-1564 *Pietà Rondanini* (Castello Sforzesco, Milano)

1555 The new pope Paul IV confirmed him in office as architect of the Works of San Pietro / Der neue Papst Paul IV bestätigt ihn als Architekt des neuen Petersdoms / Le nouveau pape Paul VI lui confirme la charge d'architecte de la Fabrique de Saint-Pierre / De nieuwe Paus, Paulus IV, stelt hem aan als architect voor de Bouwwerkzaamheden van de Sint-Pieter

---

Andrea Palladio

Padova 1508 - Maser, Treviso 1580

1521-1522 Padova: Apprenticed to Bartolomeo cavazza / Lehrling bei Bartolomeo Cavazza / Apprentissage chez Bartolomeo Cavazza / Leerling bij Bartolomeo Cavazza

c. 1530 Studied humanism with Giorgio Trissino / Humanistische Ausbildung bei Giorgio Trissino / Formation humaniste auprès de Giorgio Trissino / Sluit zich bij Giorgio Trissino aan bij het Humanisme

1542 Villa Valmarana, Vigardolo (Vicenza)

1549-1555 La Basilica, Vicenza

1551-1557 Palazzo Chiericati, Vicenza

1554 Roma. Villa Barbaro, Maser (Treviso)

1555 Villa Foscari ("la Malcontenta"), Mira (Venezia)

1558 Villa Emo, Fanzolo (Treviso)

1566-1567 La Rotonda, Vicenza; San Giorgio Maggiore, Venezia

1570 Published his treatise *The Four Books of Architecture* / Er veröffentlicht das *Traktat über die Vier Bücher zur Architektur* / Public son traité des *Quattro libri dell'architettura* / Publiceert de verhandeling over I quattro libri dell'architettura (De vier boeken over de architectuur)

1574 Bologna, San Petronio: Studies for the façade / Studien für die Fassade / Étude pour la façade / Studies voor de voorgevel

1577-1592 Il Redentore, Venezia

1580 Teatro Olimpico, Vicenza

Piero della Francesca

Borgo San Sepolcro, Arezzo 1415/20- 1492

1439-1440 Firenze: Apprenticed to Domenico Veneziano / Schüler von Domenico Veneziano / Il est l'élève de Domenico Veneziano / Is leerling van Domenico Veneziano

1440-1445 *Baptism of Christ / Taufe Christi / Baptême du Christ / Doop van Christus* (National Gallery, London)

1445 *Polyptych of Mercy / Polyptychon des Mitleids / Polyptyque de la Miséricorde / Veelluik van de Misericordia* (Pinacoteca, Borgo San Sepolcro)

1449 Ferrara: Guest of the Estense Family / Aufenthalt bei der Familie d'Este / Séjour chez les Este / Verblijft aan het hof van d'Este

1451 Rimini: Summoned by Sigismondo Malatesta, met Leon Battista Alberti and painted the fresco in the Tempio Malatestiano / Er wird von Sigismondo Malatesta gerufen, trifft Leon Battista Alberti und malt das Fresko im Tempio Malatestiano / Appelé par Sigismondo Malatesta, rencontre Leon Battista Alberti et réalise les fresques dans le Tempio Malatestiano / Wordt opgeroepen door Sigismondo Malatesta, ontmoet Leon Battista Alberti en verwezenlijkt het fresco in de Tempio Malatestiano

1452-1460 Arezzo, San Francesco: *Legend of the True Cross / Legende des wahren Kreuzes / Histoire de la Vraie Croix / Legende van het Ware Kruis*

1453 Arezzo

1455 *Flagellation / Die Geißelung Christi / Flagellation / Geseling* (Galleria Nazionale delle Marche, Urbino)

1459 Roma

c. 1460 *Madonna del Parto / Madonna der Geburt / Madonna van de Bevalling* (Museo della Madonna del Parto, Monterchi)

1463 *Resurrection / Auferstehung Christi / Résurrection / Wederopstanding* (Pinacoteca Comunale, Sansepolcro)

c. 1465 *Portraits of Federico da Montefeltro and Battista Sforza / Bildnisse von Federico da Montefeltro und Battista Sforza / Portraits de Federico da Montefeltro et de Battista Sforza / Portretten van Federico da Montefeltro en Battista Sforza* (Galleria degli Uffizi, Firenze)
1472-1474 *Brera Altarpiece / Der Brera Altar / Retable de Brera / Altaarstuk van Brera* (Pinacoteca di Brera, Milano)
1473 *De prospectiva pingendi; De quinque corporibus regularibus*

Raffaello Sanzio
Urbino 1483 - Roma 1520
1502-1503 Siena, Libreria Piccolomini: Provided some drawings to Pinturicchio for the fresco cycle dedicated to *Stories of Enea Silvio Piccolomini* / Er liefert Pinturicchio einige Zeichnungen für Fresken mit den *Geschichten von Äneas Silvio Piccolomini* / Fournit au Pinturicchio quelques cartons pour les fresques de l'*Histoire d'Enea Silvio Piccolomini* / Levert aan Pinturicchio een aantal ontwerpen voor de fresco's met de *Geschiedenis van Eneas Silvius Piccolomini*
1503-1505 Perugia: *Mond Crucifixion / Kreuzigung Mond / Crucifixion Mond / Mond Kruisiging* (National Gallery, London); *Oddi Altarpiece / Der Oddi Altar / Retable Oddi / Oddi Altaarstuk* (Pinacoteca Vaticana, Roma)
1504 *Marriage of the Virgin / Vermählung der Maria / Mariage de la Vierge / Huwelijk van de Maagd* (Pinacoteca di Brera, Milano)
1504-1508 Resided in Florence and also travelled to Perugia and Urbino / Aufenthalt in Florenz, von wo aus er auch nach Perugia und Urbino reist / Séjourne à Florence et se rend de là à Pérouse et à Urbino / Verblijft in Florence van waaruit hij ook Perugia en Urbino bezoekt
1505-1506 *Ansidei Altarpiece / Ansidei Altar / Retable Ansidei / Ansidei Altaarstuk* (National Gallery, London)
1507 *Baglioni Deposition / Kreuzabnahme Baglioni / Retable Baglioni / Kruisafneming Baglioni* (Galleria Borghese, Roma)
1508-1511 Stanza della Segnatura
1509 Roma: Summoned by Julius II to participate in painting the decorations for his apartment in the Palazzi Vaticani / Er wird von Papst Julius II gerufen, um an der Dekoration seiner Wohnräume in den Palazzi Vaticani teilzunehmen / Il est appelé par le pape Jules II pour participer à la décoration picturale de ses appartements du Vatican / Wordt opgeroepen door Paus Julius II om deel te nemen aan het decoreren van zijn woning in het Palazzi Vaticani
1511-1514 Stanza di Eliodoro
1512 Villa Farnesina: *Triumph of Galatea / Ausführung der Galatea / Galatée / Verwezenlijkt de Galatea*
1514 Succeeded to Bramante as director of the Works of San Pietro / Er übernimmt nach Bramante die Leitung der Arbeiten am neuen Petersdom / Succède à Bramante à la direction de la Fabrique de Saint-Pierre / Neemt na Bramante de leiding over de bouwwerkzaamheden van de Sint-Pieter
1514-1517 Stanza dell'Incendio. Cartoons for the *Acts of the Apostles* tapestries for the Cappella Sistina in the Vatican / Teppichkartone mit den *Leben der Apostel* für die Sixtinische Kapelle im Vatikan / Cartons pour les tapisseries des *Actes des Apôtres* pour la chapelle Sixtine / Kartons voor de wandtapijten met de *Handelingen der Apostelen* voor de Sixtijnse Kapel in het Vaticaan
1516 Palazzi Vaticani: Decorated the Loggetta and Stufetta painting for cardinal Bibbiena / Für Kardinal Bibbiena dekoriert er die Loggetta und die Stufetta / Exécute pour le cardinal Bibbiena la décoration de la Loggetta et de la Stufetta / Voert, voor kardinaal Bibbiena, de decoraties uit voor de Loggetta en voor de Stufetta
1517 *Transfiguration / Trasfiguration / Transfiguratie* (Pinacoteca Vaticana, Roma)
1518 Loggia di Psiche, La Farnesina

Tiziano Vecellio
Pieve di Cadore c. 1490 - Venezia 1576
1508 Venezia, Fondaco dei Tedeschi: frescoed the lateral façade / Fresken für die Seitenfassade / Fresque de la façade latérale / Brengt fresco's aan op de voorgevel
1511 Padova, Scuola del Santo: Frescos with the three miracles of St. Anthony / Fresken mit den drei

Wundern des Hl. Antonius / Fresques avec les trois miracles de saint Antoine / Fresco's met de drie wonderen van de Heilige Antonius

1513 Roma: Invited by Leo X / Er wird von Papst Leo X. gerufen / Il est invité par le pape Léon X / Wordt uitgenodigd door Paus Leo X

1514 Venezia: *Sacred and Profane Love / Himmlische und irdische Liebe / Amour sacré et amour profane / Hemelse en Aardse Liefde* (Galleria Borghese, Roma)

1516-1518 *Assumption of the Virgin / Himmelfahrt Mariä / Assomption de la Vierge / Maria-Tenhemelopneming* (Santa Maria Gloriosa de' Frari, Venezia)

1518 Various visits to duke Alfonso I d'Este in Ferrara / Verschiedene Aufenthalte in Ferrara beim Herzog Alfonso I. d'Este / Divers séjours à Ferrare, chez le duc Alphonse Ier d'Este / Verschillende verblijven in Ferrara bij graaf Alfonso I d 'Este

1518-1524 *Bacchanal* for the room of Alfonso I d'Este / *Bacchanal* für die Kammer von Alfonso I. d'Este / *Bacchanales* pour la chambre d'Alphonse Ier d'Este / *Bacchanalia* voor de kamer van Alfonso I d'Este

1520-1522 *Averoldi Polyptych / Polyptychon Averoldi / Polyptyque Averoldi / Averoldi Veelluik* (Santi Nazaro e Celso, Brescia)

1523 Ferrara: Finished the second painting for the room of Alfonso, *Bacchus and Ariadne* / Zweites Bild für die Kammer von Alfonso, *Bacchus und Ariadne* / Exécute le second tableau pour la chambre d'Alphonse Ier d'Este, *Bacchus et Ariane* / Verwezenlijkt het tweede schilderij voor de kamer van Alfonso, *Bacchus en Ariadne* (National Gallery, London)

1530 First portrait of Charles V / Erstes Portrait Karl V. / Premier portrait de Charles Quint / Eerste portret van Karel V

1536-1538 Portraits of *Francesco Maria della Rovere* and *Eleonora Gonzaga* / Portraits von *Francesco Maria della Rovere* und *Eleonora Gonzaga* / Portraits de *Francesco Maria della Rovere* et *d'Eleonora Gonzaga* / Portretten van *Francesco Maria della Rovere* en *Eleonora Gonzaga* (Galleria degli Uffizi, Firenze)

1538 *Venus* (Galleria degli Uffizi, Firenze)

1540 Began to paint the *Crowning with Thorns* / Er beginnt mit dem Christus mit der Dornenkrone / Commence à peindre le *Couronnement d'épines* / Begint met het schilderen van de *Christus met de Doornenkroon* (Musée du Louvre, Parigi)

1543 *Ecce Homo* (Kunsthistorisches Museum, Wien)

1548 Travelled to Augsburg at the invitation of Charles V / Auf Einladung Karl V. kommt er nach Augsburg / Il se rend à Augsbourg à l'invitation de Charles Quint / Bereikt Augsburg op uitnodiging van Karel V; *Portrait of Charles V at the Battle of Mühlberg / Portrait von Karl V in der Schlacht zu Mühlberg / Portrait de Charles Quint à la bataille de Mühlberg / Portret van Karel V bij de slag bij Mühlberg* (Museo del Prado, Madrid)

1551 Venezia: Elected brother of the Scuola di San Rocco / Mitbruder der Schule San Rocco / Il est reçu dans la confrérie de la Scuola di San Rocco / Wordt gekozen tot confrère van de Scuola di San Rocco

1554 Sent the *Holy Trinity* to Charles V / Tizian schickt Karl V. die *Trinität* / Il envoie à Charles Quint la *Trinità* / Titiaan stuurt Karel V de *Drie-eenheid* (Museo del Prado, Madrid)

1565 Sent the *Last Supper* to Spain / Er schickt *Das Letzte Abendmahl* nach Spanien / Expédie en Espagne la *Cène* / Hij stuurt het *Laatste Avondmaal* naar Spanje (Escorial)

Rogier van der Weyden

Tournai *c.* 1400 - Bruxelles 1464

1427 Apprenticed to Robert Campin / Schüler von Robert Campin / Élève de Robert Campin / Leerling van Robert Campin

1432 Tournai: Nominated a free master of painting / Er wird zum freien Meister der Malerei ernannt / Il est nommé maître à la Guilde de peinture / Wordt benoemd tot vrije meester van de schilderkunst in Doornik

1432-1435 *Portrait of a Lady / Bildnis eines jungen Mädchens / Portrait de jeune femme / Portret van een jong meisje* (National Gallery of Art, Washington)

1436-1437 Bruxelles: Nominated official painter of the city / Offizieller Maler der Stadt / Il est nommé peintre officiel de la ville / Wordt uitgeroepen tot officiële stadsschilder

1450 Travelled to Italy for the Jubilee / Reise nach Italien zum Jubiläum / Voyage en Italie pour le Jubilé / Reist naar Italië voor het Jublieum; *Portrait of Francesco d'Este / Portrait von Francesco d'Este / Portrait de François d'Este / Portret van Francesco d'Este* (Metropolitan Museum of Art, New York)

1456 *Crucifixion / Große Kreuzigung / Grande Crucifixion / Grote Kruisiging* (San Lorenzo de El Escorial, Madrid)

Jan van Eyck

Maastricht c. 1390 - Brugge 1441

1422-1424 Den Haag

1425 Nominated court painter of the duke of Borgogne / Hofmaler beim Herzog von Burgund / Il est nommé peintre officiel du duc de Bourgogne / Wordt benoemd tot hofschilder van de Hertog van Borgogna

1425-1427 *Madonna with Canon Van der Paele / Madonna des Kanonikus Van der Paele / Vierge au chanoine Van der Paele / Madonna met kanunnik Joris van der Paele* (Musée des Beaux-Arts, Brugge)

1428 Lisboa: Diplomatic mission / Diplomatische Mission / Mission diplomatique / Diplomatieke missie

1432 Brugge: *Polyptych of the Mystic Lamb/ Polyptychon des mystischen Lamms / Retable de l'Agneau mystique/ Veelluik "Het Lam Gods"* (Saint Bavon, Gent)

1433 *Man with a Red Turban / Mann mit rotem Turban / L'Homme au turban rouge / Man met de rode tulband* (National Gallery, London)

1434 *The Arnolfini Portrait / Die Arnolfini-Hochzeit / Arnolfini et sa femme (ou Portrait des époux Arnolfini) / Portret van Giovanni Arnolfini en zijn vrouw* (National Gallery, London)

1434-1435 *Rolin Madonna / Madonna des Kanzlers Rolin / Vierge au chancelier Rolin / Madonna met Kanselier Rolin* (Musée du Louvre, Paris)

Glossary
Glossar
Glossaire
Verklarende Woordenlijst

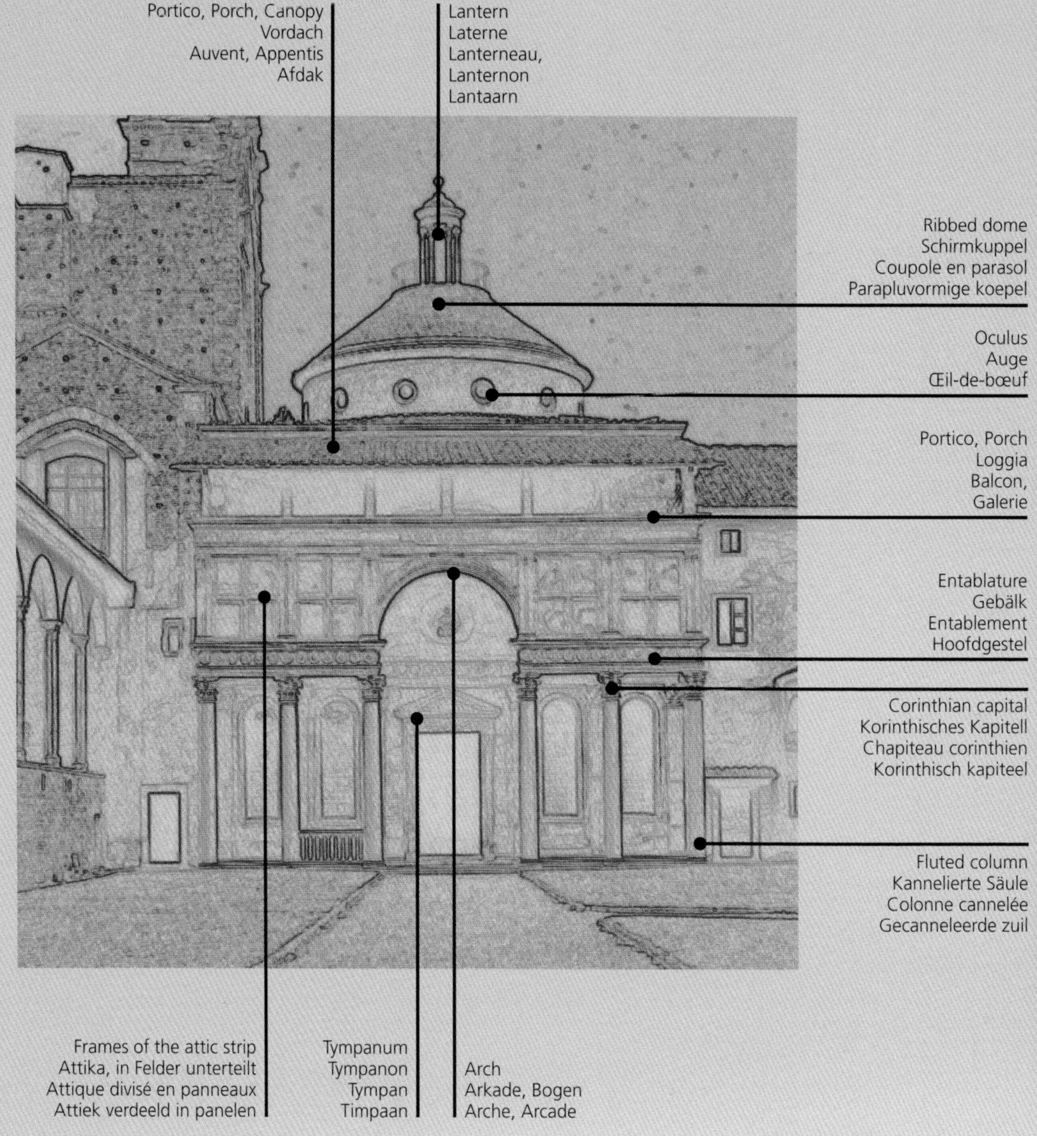

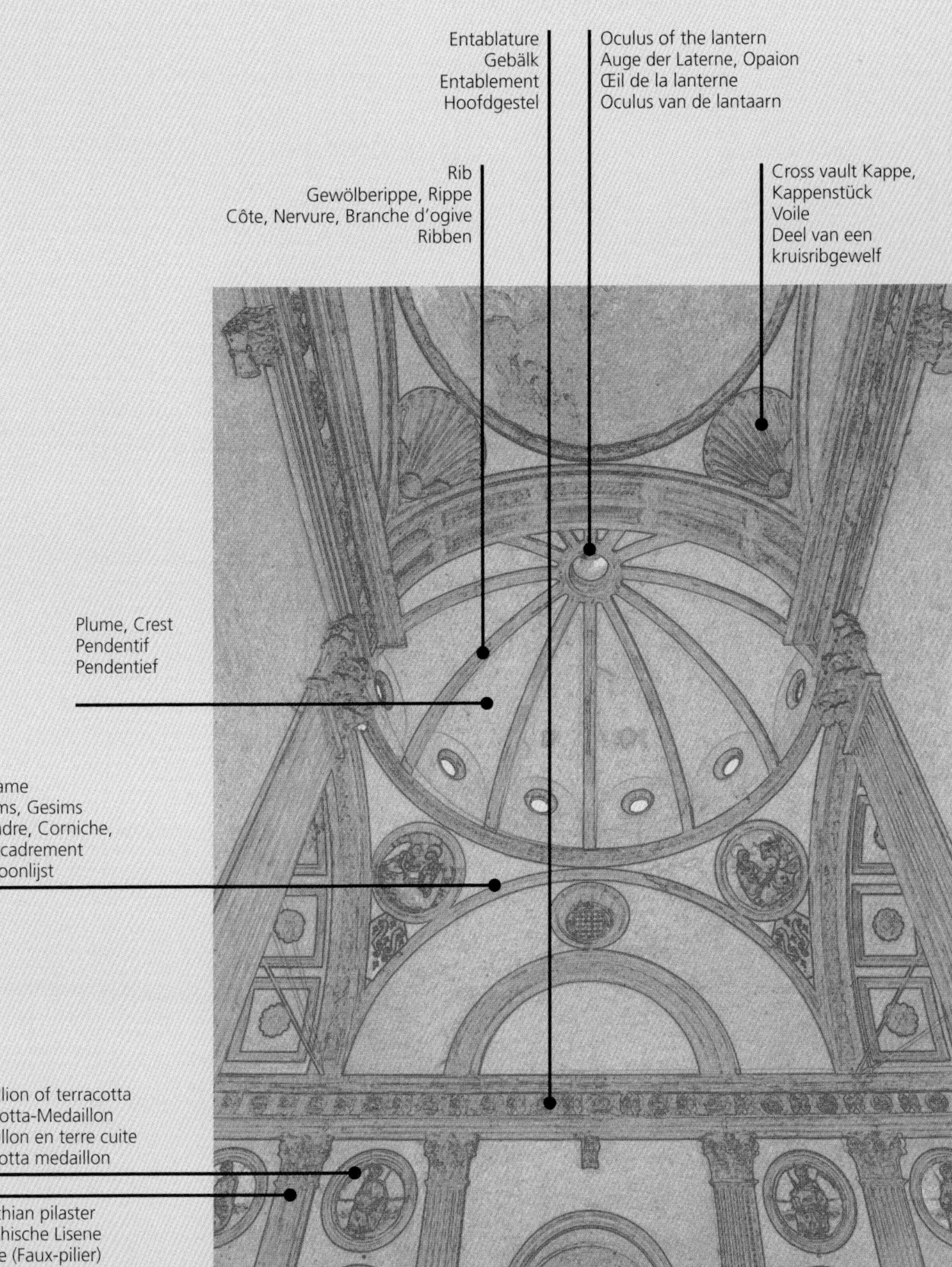
Entablature
Gebälk
Entablement
Hoofdgestel
Oculus of the lantern
Auge der Laterne, Opaion
Œil de la lanterne
Oculus van de lantaarn
Rib
Gewölberippe, Rippe
Côte, Nervure, Branche d'ogive
Ribben
Cross vault Kappe,
Kappenstück
Voile
Deel van een
kruisribgewelf
Plume, Crest
Pendentif
Pendentief
Frame
Sims, Gesims
Cadre, Corniche,
Encadrement
Kroonlijst
Medallion of terracotta
Terrakotta-Medaillon
Médaillon en terre cuite
Terracotta medaillon
Corinthian pilaster
Korinthische Lisene
Pilastre (Faux-pilier)
corinthien
Korinthische liseen

Monumental cornice
Gesims
Cadre, Corniche, Encadrement
Kroonlijst

Halfpediment,
Open pediment
Halber Tympanon
Faux -tympan
Half-timpaan

Frieze
Fries
Frise

Inscription
Inschrift
Inscriptie

Pediment, Tympanum
Tympanon
Tympan
Timpaan

Fluted pilaster
Kannelierter Pilaster, Kannelierter Halb-oder Wandp
Pilastre (Faux-pilier) cannelé
Gecanneleerde half-brugpijler

Oculus
Auge
Œil-de-bœuf

Capital
Kapitell
Chapiteau
Kapiteel

Socle
Sockel
Plinthe,
Soubassement
Voetstuk

Half-column
Blendsäule
Colonne engagée
Halfzuil

Plinth
Basis
Base, Embasement, Semelle, Socle, Soubassement
Fundering

Blind arch
Blendarkade,
Wandarkade
Arcade aveugle
Blinde arcade

Bracket
Konsole, Kra
Console, Tro
Kraagsteen

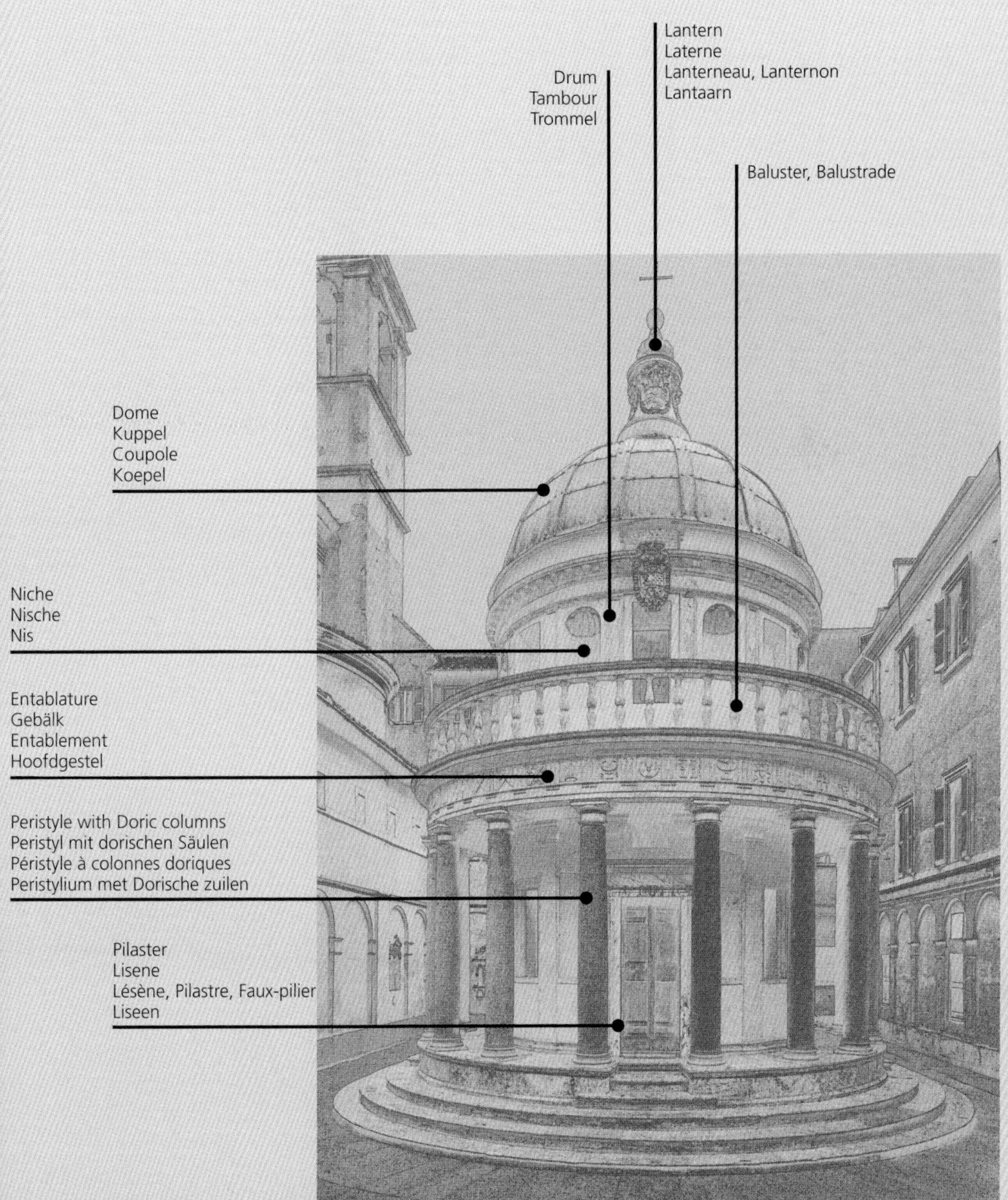
Lantern
Laterne
Lanterneau, Lanternon
Lantaarn
Drum
Tambour
Trommel
Baluster, Balustrade
Dome
Kuppel
Coupole
Koepel
Niche
Nische
Nis
Entablature
Gebälk
Entablement
Hoofdgestel
Peristyle with Doric columns
Peristyl mit dorischen Säulen
Péristyle à colonnes doriques
Peristylium met Dorische zuilen
Pilaster
Lisene
Lésène, Pilastre, Faux-pilier
Liseen

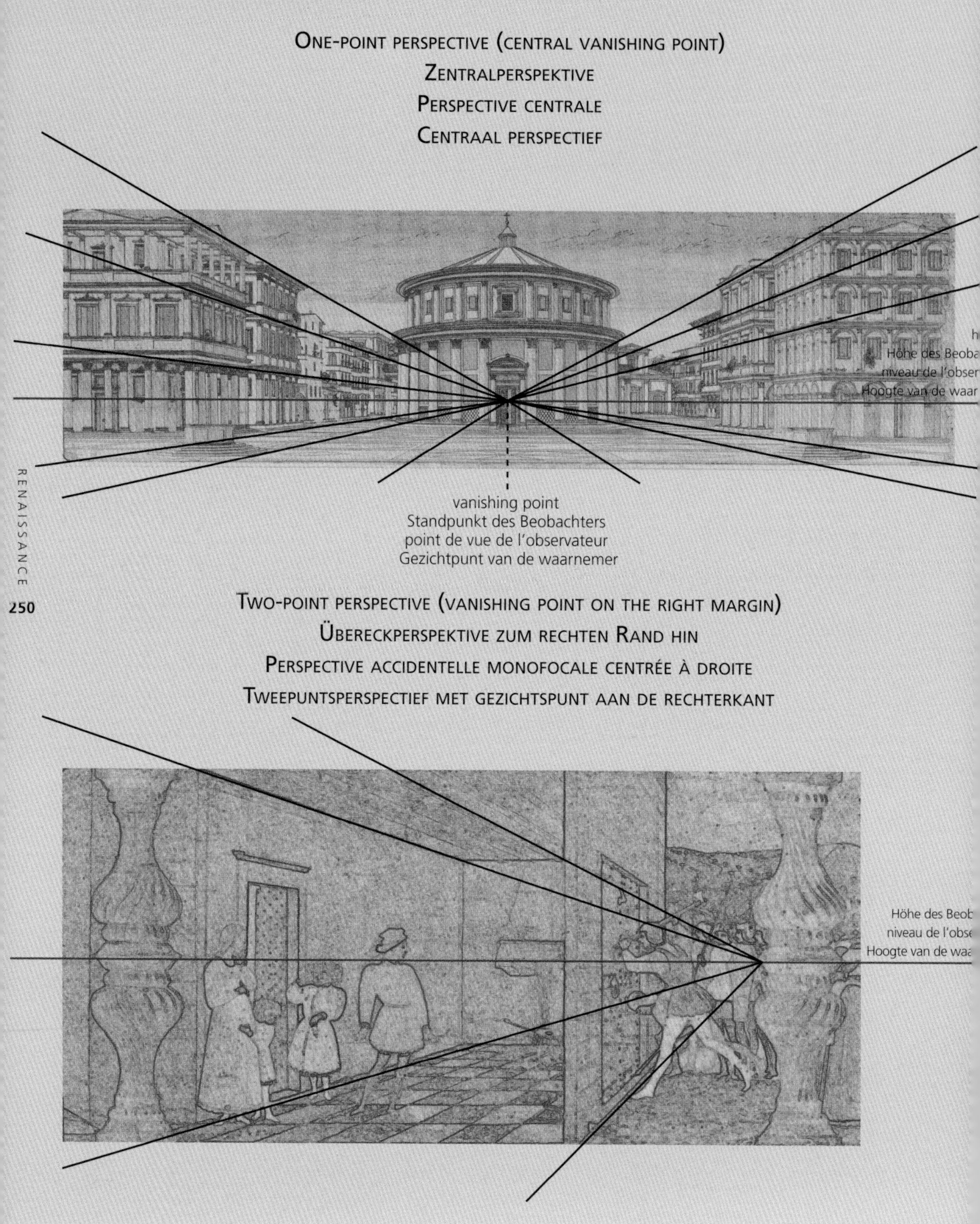
One-point perspective (central vanishing point)
Zentralperspektive
Perspective centrale
Centraal perspectief
vanishing point
Standpunkt des Beobachters
point de vue de l'observateur
Gezichtpunt van de waarnemer
Two-point perspective (vanishing point on the right margin)
Übereckperspektive zum rechten Rand hin
Perspective accidentelle monofocale centrée à droite
Tweepuntsperspectief met gezichtspunt aan de rechterkant

Three-point perspective (two lateral and one central vanishing points)
Übereckperspektive mit zwei seitlichen äusseren Fluchtpunkten und einem zentralen
Perspective accidentelle à deux point de fuite latéraux et un central
Tweepuntsperspectief met twee laterale externe gezichtspunten en één centraal gezichtspunt

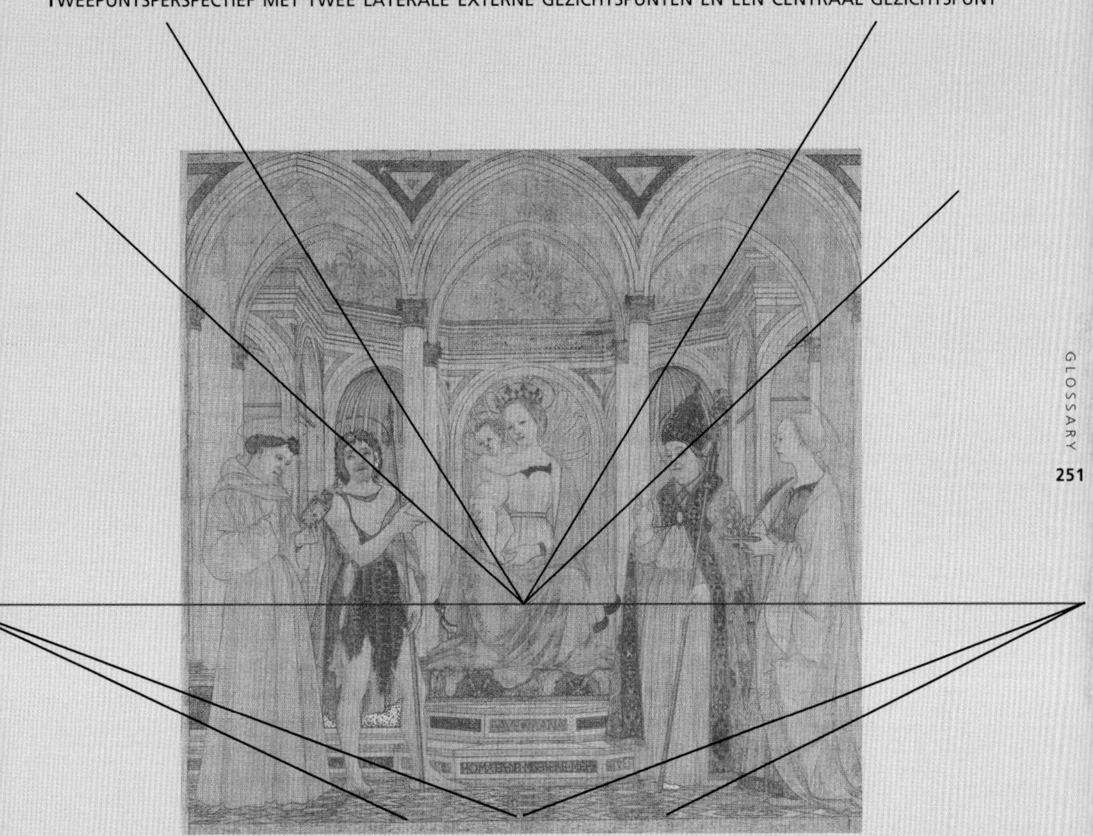

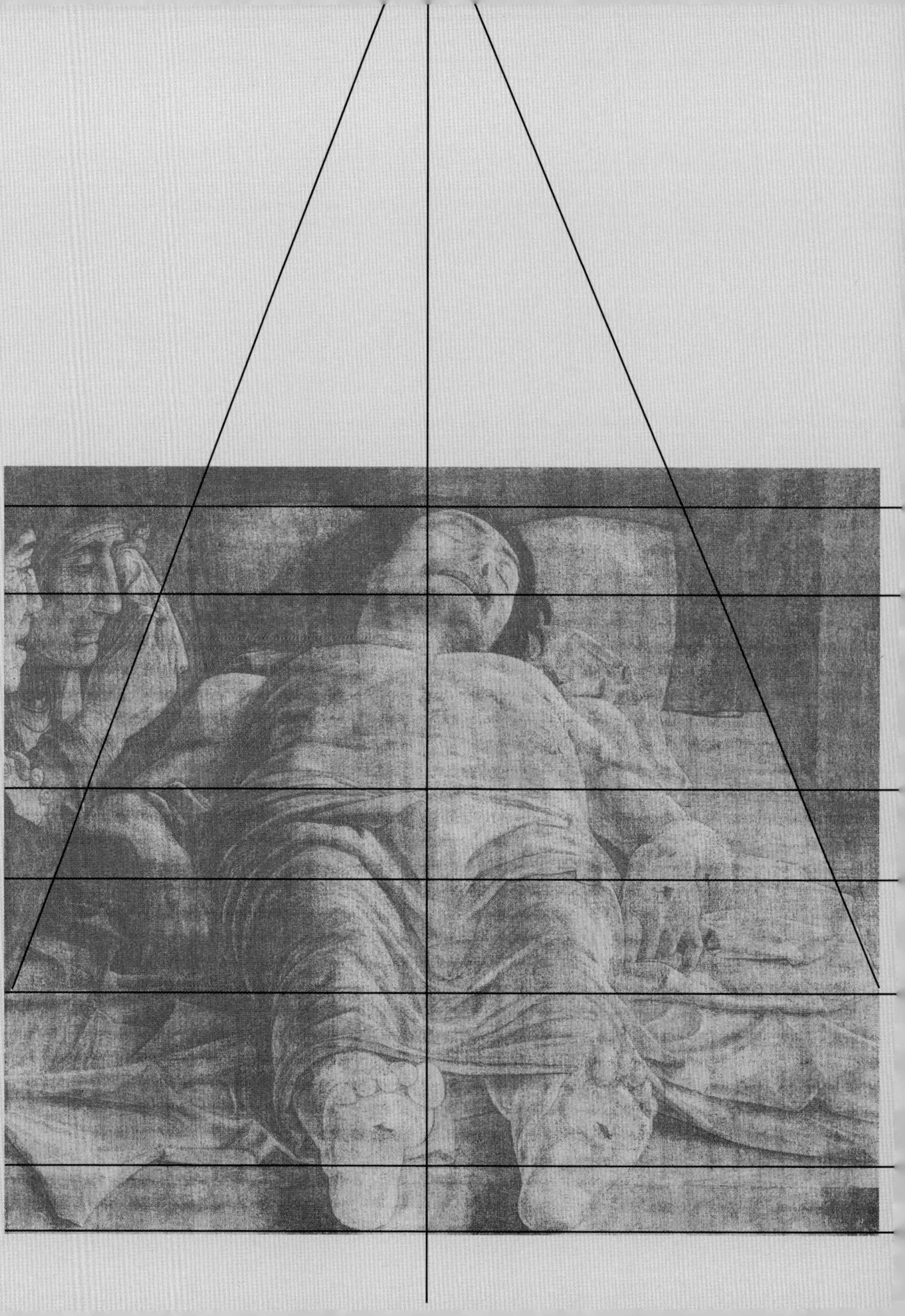

Axonometric projection
Perspektivische Verkürzung mit Axonometrie
Vue perspective axonométrique
Perspectivische verkorting met axonometrisch perspectief

Renaissance Art in European Museums
Museen der Renaissancekunst in Europa
Musées d'art Renaissance en Europe
Musea van de renaissancekunst in Europa

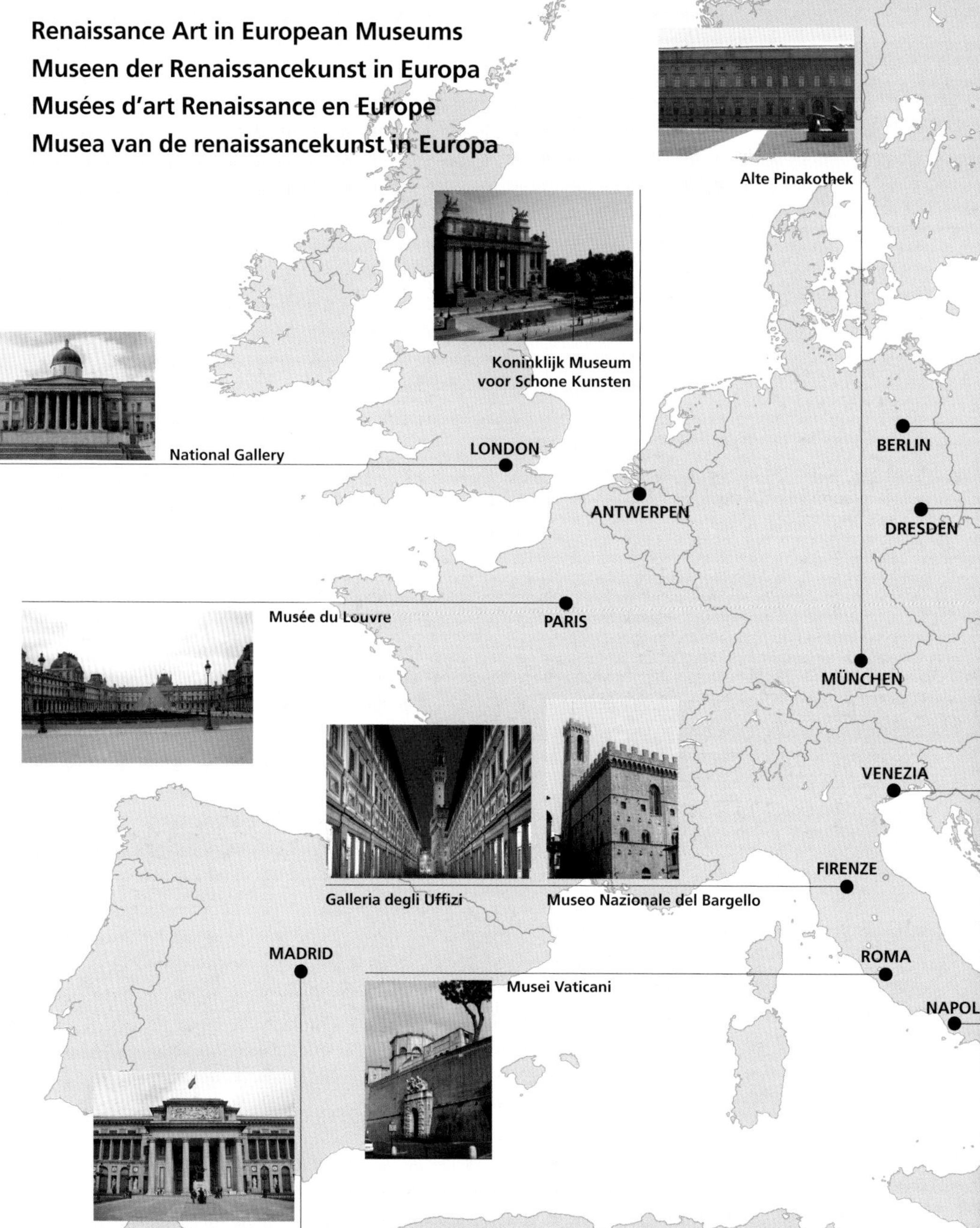

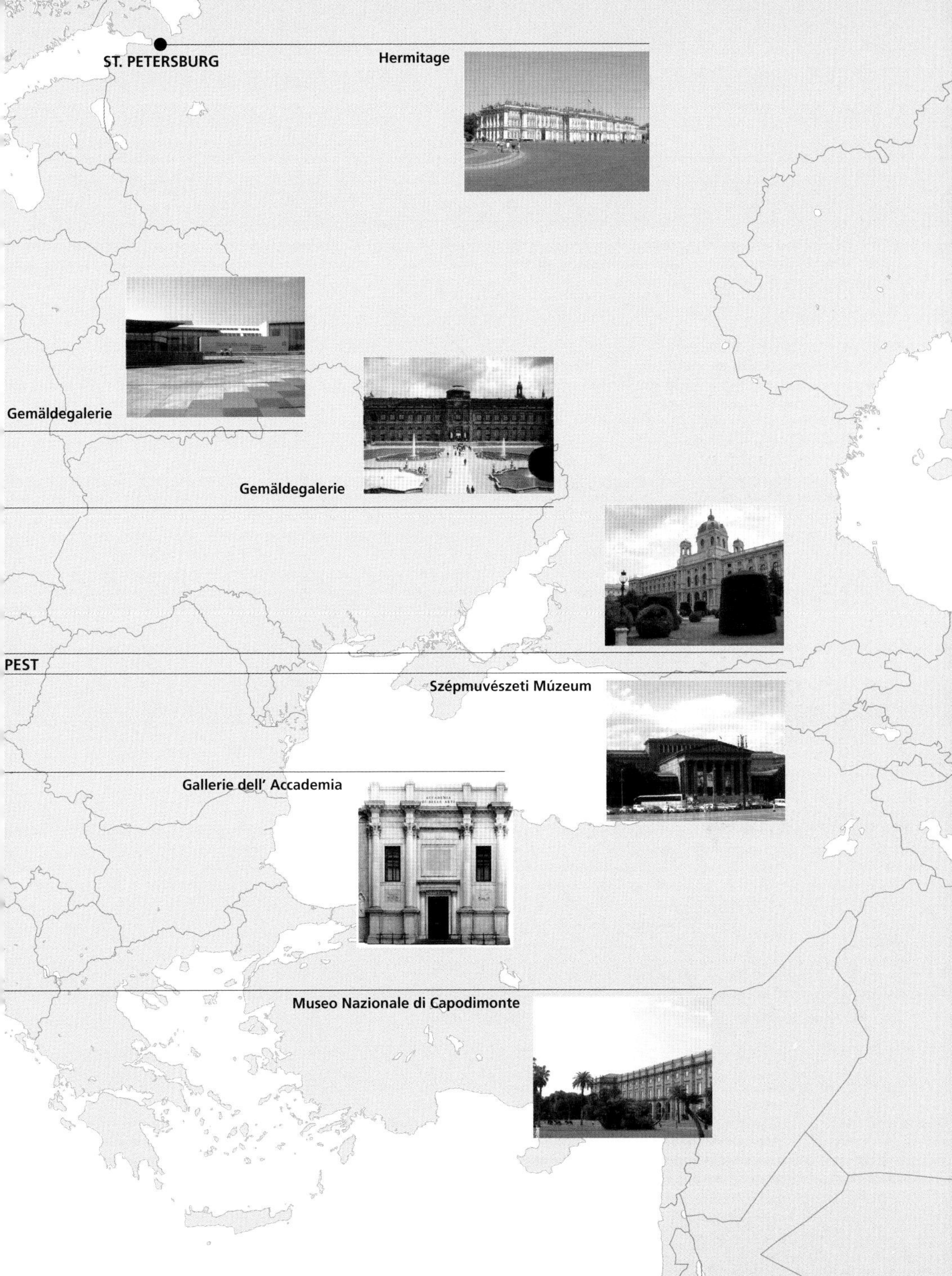

ST. PETERSBURG
Hermitage
Gemäldegalerie
Gemäldegalerie
PEST
Szépmuvészeti Múzeum
Gallerie dell' Accademia
Museo Nazionale di Capodimonte

62, via Chiantigiana
50012 Bagno a Ripoli
Florence (Italy)

Text and picture research: Shaaron Magrelli, Angela Sanna, Francesca Taddei

English translation: Johanna Kreiner
French translation: Denis-Armand Canal

Printed in China 2011

ISBN (English): 978-88-6637-084-0
ISBN (German): 978-88-6637-083-3
ISBN (Dutch): 978-88-6637-085-7

Created and distributed in cooperation with Frechmann Kolón GmbH
www.frechmann.com

Project Management: E-ducation.it S.p.A. Firenze